Rin

WITHDRAWN

Get **more** out of libraries

Please return or renew this item by the last date shown.

You can renew online at www.hants.gov.uk/library

Or by phoning 0300 555 1387

Hampshire
County Council

Myddle

The life and times of a
Shropshire farmworker's
daughter 1911-1928

HELEN EBREY

MERLIN UNWIN BOOKS

Note: We have not attempted to translate the old pounds, shillings ('s') and pence ('d') into modern money. 6d could be rendered as 2½p, but that would be totally meaningless in terms of purchasing power. Suffice it to say that prior to 1971, 12 pennies were a shilling, and 20 shillings equalled £1. One shilling and six pence might be written 1/6d. In the narrative a farm labourer only earns 12s 6d per week, and a cottage sells for £90 while another is thought too high-priced at £140 – so it would be quite unrealistic to interrupt the story with modern-day equivalents of the old coinage.

Disclaimer: The residents recorded in this book are in no way connected with any present-day owners or occupiers of Helen's home over 90 years ago, or of those in any other properties.

Acknowledgements

I would like to thank the many people in and around Myddle who helped my mother and myself, over the years, during preparation of her childhood story - in some cases, replying in detail to my various queries that arose from my mother's telling of her story.

I also wish to thank the Local Studies Department, Shropshire County Libraries; Janice V. Cox for the photo of Webscott Chapel; page 111.

Drawings (pages 12, 44, 46, 124 and 147) are of local scenes in the 1980s by myself.

I have made use of the following books in my research:

The History of Myddle Richard Gough (1701)
The Buildings of England (Shropshire) Nikolaus Pevsner
We are Seven William Wordsworth
A Short History of the Church and Parish of St. Peter's, Myddle, Shropshire E.M.W. Rogers 1984
An English Rural Community – Myddle under the Tudors and Stuarts David G Hey, MA, PhD

Elizabeth Brown

Richard Gough's *History of Myddle* (1701) and Helen Ebrey's *Myddle* (2016)

Around 300 years before Helen related her own childhood story, Myddle resident Richard Gough wrote a remarkable, detailed account of the lives of people living in that same village at that time.

Many towns and villages throughout England are well represented in terms of our knowledge of the gentry and the most important families. But Gough put Myddle in a rare position. We not only know who occupied the Castle and the various Halls in the area, but also who did what and to whom (in incredible detail) among the local population.

So (for example) we know that poor Anne Parkes '*learned to knit stockens and gloves*' to earn her living; just as Helen's mother did in Myddle (almost three centuries later) as one of numerous ways to achieve a basic subsistence level for the family.

Likewise we discover from Gough that one '*Cooke Hayward gave £10 to the Poore of this side of the Parish of Myddle, the interest to bee dealt in bread on the first Lord's day of every month, among such poore people as come to Church to receive it*'.

But it is only from Helen that we learn that receiving such bread at Myddle Church (sometimes less fresh than it should have been!) remained an essential part of the sustenance of '*poore people*' such as her own family, well into the 1900s.

Children at Myddle School (such as Helen) probably learned that Richard Gough had been a pupil there – but not necessarily that he wrote what was to become a key work in the study of English local history, as seen from the viewpoint of ordinary folk.

If Helen Ebrey had set out to leave us a 20th-century updating of Gough's groundbreaking work, then *Myddle* might be that book.

Contents

To Helen's son Michael
(1940-1982)
who loved Myddle

CHAPTER ONE

A Twentieth Century Village Childhood

Helen Ebrey, my mother, was known locally as Nell. She spent her childhood in Myddle, Shropshire. She was born in 1911, shortly before the Great War. This is Helen's story.

My parents were poor, living in a tied farm cottage near Balderton Hall, where Father worked as a labourer. The Hall was a magnificent Elizabethan farmhouse situated on the north side of the road from Yorton to Myddle. At the period of my childhood, however, Father was more concerned where the next meal was coming from than the handsome group of buildings in which he found employment.

The cottages were in a terrace of three (we lived at No. 2) and the lane continued beyond them towards the scattered dwellings known as the hamlet of Houlston.

Father (William Henry Ebrey) was a Myddle man and Mother (Emily Davis Ebrey) came from Baschurch. Ebreys had lived in Myddle in 1758 when a Sara Ebry married Joe Davis at Myddle Church (St Peter's). They may have originally come from Wem, where records are available of various spellings of Ebrey from 1685 onwards.

To return to my early life at Balderton Cottage: I was the second child in the family, Emily (Em) being one year older. We were close friends, she being my confidante and this companionship was vital when we commenced employment together and were forced to face horrors we could never have imagined. However, I race ahead. Many years of childhood intervened before this unhappy period.

When I was four [1915] we moved from my birthplace into the very heart of Myddle. Mother had wanted to move to be near the school, church, store, pump and family members, especially Father's mother, our Granny Ebrey, who lived in the Gullet – but I return to this ancient water channel/footpath later.

Our new home in the heart of the village was 'Rose Cottage' and had previously been occupied by an Estate Bailiff. It sat on the road which continued through the pretty village on its way to Baschurch and Ruyton-XI-Towns (a river town on the River Perry, so-called because eleven townships comprise the parish).

We were proud that our village possessed a castle. Although visibly not a great deal remained, an interesting corner turret survived, with attractive, centuries-old sandstone masonry. The castle ruins were located at Castle Farm.

Our Parish Church, St. Peter's, was near Castle Farm, in the heart of the village. Much later, when Father retired, he became a church sexton and rang the bells for services from the ancient tower.

It was quite usual to see cattle on the hoof in those days. Cows were driven by shouting drovers on the occasions of the market at Shrewsbury Smithfield, the 8 miles or so along the lanes. Two working farms, Alford and Castle, occupied the village centre. Milking of cows, by hand, twice daily including Sundays brought employment to local women.

Our magnificent inn, the *Red Lion*, was built in the seventeenth century and thought originally to have been a barn belonging to Eagle Farm (now called Alford). The Inn dominated the village centre with its immense size. Much land was then appended to it (several fields in the village as well as at Myddlewood). The clubroom, over the inn stables, was the centre of business activities. Estate rents were collected here and the eventual sale of all estate property was undertaken here also. On days when the hunt met in the square in front of the inn, the sight was a colourful spectacle.

I attended the sandstone village school, which the Myddle author Richard Gough, born 1635, had also attended.

The cast-iron pump for drinking-water was in the school playground, near the road and within a low wall to keep schoolchildren away at breaks when villagers might be collecting their water.

The well or pump was the focus of village life, for it was here everyone queued for vital drinking water, and the spot where news and gossip was shared. The clanging of empty buckets was a pleasant familiar sound as folk passed our cottage on the way to collect the precious commodity.

Myddle Castle as it stood in Helen's younger years. In reality a fortified manor-house, dating from a time when Welsh incursions necessitated such structures. It fell into ruins in the 16th and 17th centuries, only this corner turret surviving to modern times. Not until the 1980s was anything done to prevent its further onslaught by wind and weather, by which time there was little left to save.

The old quarry at the end of our lane was a huge, deep hole in the ground, where sandstone had been quarried over the years. It was the place where folk threw their rubbish. We were not anxious to play here however, for fear of rats!

Rose Cottage

Our new cottage was small, homely, and constructed on lines of rudimentary simplicity. Two rooms and a tiny pantry occupied the ground floor, and access to the two bedrooms was by a dark staircase and a long, equally-dark landing. An outside wash-house built at the side of the cottage housed a log-burning boiler, and here sacks of Indian corn were stored for the hens. A generous garden extended from the back of the dwelling.

It was customary for estate cottages to be provided with a field or orchard, to encourage tenants to keep livestock, and ours was at the top of the hill behind the cottage, approached by a steeply sloping footpath from Myddle Bank.

Many exposed beams added to the character of the interior of Rose Cottage. The focal point in the living room was, without doubt, the magnificent cast-iron range, always warm and inviting, and a most pleasing object to sit near. Mother lovingly cleaned it every Saturday morning with faultless regularity. The black-leading she used was available at ½d per brick; flues at the back were cleaned out at the same time. A piece of binder twine, stretched between nails across the mantelpiece, provided a useful hanging place for damp clothes. Mother and Father each possessed an old-fashioned second-hand armchair but we children had to sit on solid straight-back wooden chairs.

Our bedroom was above the living room, with an enormous chimney-breast which warmed the room a little. A double bed occupied most of the floor space, with pretty brass bedsteads, where we hung our clothes overnight. Nails had been driven into the latch-door to hang clothes on. A large cot stood in the corner, suitable for the two smallest children. (At this point in time we were two but gradually our family increased to six children).

Mother had a special propensity to make much out of little. She made attractive warm rugs from old tweed coats and jackets acquired at jumble sales, cutting the fabric into small lengths which she pulled through a sack base with a wooden prodding tool, before knotting them. Farmers gladly gave her the sacks, and some bore the emblem of a cow or cockerel, being an advertisement. This design was often incorporated into the rug, and a border added in whatever dark shades of cloth she had. These warm rugs covered the floors, which were cold red bricks downstairs and wooden boards in the bedrooms.

We used paraffin lamps and candles for lighting, and went to bed by candle light in winter. Our cottage door was usually wide open on warm days because of the heat from the range. Passers-by would call a friendly greeting to Mother and news was regularly exchanged.

BATHTIME

Saturday evening without fail was bathnight. It was chaos and confusion when the old tin tub was carried indoors by Father from the wash-house and placed in front of the range. Mother heated water in a variety of pots and pans and soon bathtime was underway. This weekly immersion in hot water was to ensure we were clean for Sunday School. Our long hair was washed at the same time, dried, and tied in rags to encourage curls.

What may be astonishing now was that Mother then washed all our clothes in the bathwater in front of the fire, wrung them out by hand, and hung them on washing lines of binder-twine strung between the beams in the front parlour. The pieces of crude furniture we possessed were pushed out of the way, and the water dripped onto the brick floor. While the clothes dried, we wore our old coats. Usually the washing was dry enough for Mother to iron in time for the garments to be worn for afternoon Sunday School.

Meanwhile on Sunday morning, we were sent off round the village in our petticoats and coats to seek to purchase a few eggs at 1d (when our own hens were not laying). These were boiled and cut in half for dinner.

Helen's mother feeding her hens in her top field.

An observant lad once commented that I was not wearing anything under my coat. I blushed, and was glad that my sister was close at hand.

Half an egg on Sunday was a special treat. That was for dinner. After Sunday School we had tea, for which Mother always baked a fairly plain cake. I should mention that Emily and I were presented with bibles and prayer books by the Rector (Reverend S.A. Woolward) for answering religious questions at Sunday School. The presentation was made on his lawn and parents were invited.

The only meals the family ate together were on a Sunday. On other days Mother and Father ate first, while we went out to play and then we had bread and dripping (kindly donated by Mrs Colemere of the *Red Lion*) or a baked potato.

Meat was available for those who could afford it. Mr Brisbane called each week with his horse and cart, the cart having a box contraption on the back in an attempt to keep meat-flies/dust and elements off the meat. The source of his supply was his brother's farm at Webscott known as 'Brisbane the Lane'. Myddle was supplied on Fridays, in all weathers, approaching via the old quarry. Mrs Davies and Mrs Painter came with their plates, then Aunt Alice next door. Mother took her plate out next for two-penny-worth of brawn, which was all we ever purchased.

Mr Brisbane's horse was then fed from a nosebag outside our cottage, while he lifted down a great basket from the seat beside him. This he filled with the choicest joints and cuts of meat, and took this heavy basket first to Mrs Porch's home (where her maid would be expecting him), then to the shop, and then to the inn. He then returned to collect the horse and cart and drove off to Alford Farm, the Rectory and Castle Farm. I often wondered why these people couldn't come out with their plates, as we did!

BREAD

Mother purchased bread baked at Baschurch by 'Francis the Baker' who delivered once a week to the village by pony and trap. She took eight loaves which lasted a week until his next visit. Father usually took cheese sandwiches for his lunch (cheese was either 2d or 4d per lb).

I was always called at 6am to help Mother light the fire to enable a kettle to be boiled for tea, and make sandwiches etc.

*****

To return to the cottage: window sills were frequently crowded with plants as geraniums, cactus and ferns all competed for what little light penetrated through the tiny windows. Ours were no exception, but the leafy greenery afforded us some small element of privacy when we all washed for school in an enamel bowl on the scrubbed whitewood table placed under the window.

Later on, when we were older, our ablutions (for some reason not at all obvious to me at the time) were performed out in the wash-house, or in the garden. In the latter case, a small section of high stone wall near the cottage offered a degree of shelter from the public gaze. We used chilled rainwater from the butt, first skimming the usual assortment of dead insects from the surface with our bowl-dish, which we then placed on an old school bench standing under the wall and acting as a washstand. Very occasionally a little square of green household soap cut from a larger slab might be available.

Our toilet was a small bucket closet in a brick hut at the top of the garden, built by the estate shortly before we moved to Rose Cottage, to replace an earlier earth closet. During warmer months it buzzed with a common selection of flies, and we were constantly harassed by large blowflies. The pigsty was part of the same building, but later Father moved the pigs into the orchard. The *Wellington Journal* served as toilet paper.

On wet days, we threw an old coat, from the back door, over our shoulders and ran, water dripping down upon us from the many knotty damson trees which lined the path. Our garden and closet were somewhat exposed to public view from the road. The degree of this exposure became more embarrassingly apparent to us when we grew a little older and big red service buses appeared on the scene. These came with faces which peered and sometimes even smiled at us when we answered the calls of nature, for there was no disguising our destination.

Politics

During a period prior to a general election the conservative agent called throughout the village enquiring if anyone would be prepared to allow a room to be rented for the day of the poll. A committee room was required and they needed somewhere close to the school while polling took place. Mother agreed to allow our front parlour to be used. The remote village fell under the Ellesmere Estates of Lord Brownlow.

Mother, in a sudden flash of inspiration, wrote to the Estate Office saying that as the room was to be used by the Conservative Party, was there any possibility of it being redecorated? (The years of hanging wet washing here to dry in time for Sunday School had taken their toll). Mother's mention of the political party involved had a remarkable influence, producing the surprising result of a decorator being sent along post-haste with rolls of paper and paint. Soon Mr Davis, the decorator for the Estate, set to work. The paper had a white background with chandeliers of red, in fact, it resembled bedroom paper, but we children loved it, and it smartened the room immediately.

The Conservative candidate was a 'Bridgewater' of Oswestry. It was a foregone conclusion that the conservative would win, because local people were fearful of their jobs on the estate and cottages and rents, if they voted any other way.

CHAPTER TWO

Childhood Fun and Games

We often played in the Rector's Coppice, approached by an ancient walled track which ran between Myddle Bank and the Lower Road. This coppice was quite a walk from the Rectory, being at the opposite end of the village. But it was an exciting playground for us with many rocky outcrops behind which we could hide.

We knew where to find some old inscribed headstones, placed in the coppice by past rectors in memory of departed pet dogs. I can remember one, which as far as we could read [the inscription being rather weathered] was dedicated to a dog called Sam who died in 1857, aged 13 years. This was at a time when deceased members of most village families were buried in the churchyard in unmarked graves [the Church of England owned much land in the village then]. The coppice was also an ideal location from which to view the castle, because it was in an elevated position, with sweeping views across the fields to Castle Farm. I suppose strictly speaking we were trespassing, but we played here often without hindrance; people didn't seem to mind in those days, and we did no damage.

Father acquired an odd 4-wheeled truck of the type which might have been used in a Welsh slate quarry. The new acquisition provided the means of moving hitherto impossibly heavy weights and bulky objects around. Goodness knows where it came from!

We used it to fetch coal from Yorton Station siding, which was a cheaper way to purchase it (at 1s 4d per sack). The journey to the station was most enjoyable. When the high sandstone wall was reached, on the stretch from Balderton Hall to Newton, one child pulled the truck, while the others jumped up onto the wall and ran along the top. This we always did as it was one of the special pleasures of walking to Yorton. Upon reaching the top of the hill near the site of St. Mary's Monastery, we all four children sat inside the truck, gradually gaining speed down a very steep hill. It's a miracle we were never involved in a serious accident; the truck had no brakes. A right turn into the station yard, and the goods siding and coal merchant's office were on the left. On warm days we sought shelter from the sun on a seat placed under a leafy weeping tree in the attractive platform garden which was kept neat and trim by the resident station-master.

The children had to push sacks of coal two miles home from Yorton station, to save the cost of having it delivered! When the Queen arrived in the 1920s to stay at Shotton Hill, this unassuming structure had been built for her possible use, doubtless bedecked with flags and bunting.

Helen's birthplace was Balderton Hall Cottages near Myddle.

Our visit to the station was never complete without a peep inside the ladies' waiting room and closet, the only water closet we had ever seen. We usually squabbled over who should pull the chain! The oddly-shaped porcelain Victorian closet-bowl was eyed with wonder, as was the dark polished wooden seat. The walls were covered with blue Delft tiles in a delicate floral design.

Eventually we concluded the business which had brought us thus far, the eldest child handing over the money for the sack of coal.

The journey home took several hours and was planned with precision. At the bottom of the hill we took off some large lumps of coal, and one of us stayed with this at the side of the lane. The others pulled the truck to the top of the hill. They then took off the sack, and one of us would mind the sack, while the others went back to fetch the coal we had taken off. This was the worst part of the journey; for other, smaller hills we all pushed and pulled hard. We were usually exhausted when we eventually arrived home.

Thus we saved Mother the delivery charge on coal brought by cart, and she needed every penny.

We assisted with the shopping. Mother's purchases were recorded in a book – farmworkers' wives did not have ready money every day, but paid their accounts after pay-day at the end of the week. If children were sent to settle their parents' accounts, the shopkeeper rewarded them with a small conical packet of sweets.

The arrival of a fairground roundabout in the village caused great excitement. It was sited near the inn, so children living in the direction of our cottage had the added pleasure of passing the apparatus, and glimpsing colourful sections projecting from beneath the rough tarpaulin cover on the way to school. The early evening sound of music wafting through the neighbourhood signalled that the roundabout was finally ready for business, and brought children hurrying from all directions to the inn.

What we saw was quite unbelievable – the most magnificent wooden horses, embellished with carvings of roses and scrolls; some were open-mouthed with lovely pearly teeth. There were gold-painted poles, rather like barley-sugar twists, affixed to each horse, which the children held on to tightly while riding round. I should have loved a ride but Mother could not manage the 1d for all of us. Instead we stood and watched while a dark-skinned man turned this amazing roundabout by hand; we heard the same tunes played over and over again, indeed long after our bedtime the rhythms filled our room and eventually lulled us happily to sleep. One evening a farmer from Myddlewood brought his two daughters for a ride and generously paid for all the watching children to have a turn – which was how I got my ride on the roundabout.

Good Friday each year was a specially memorable time for us. After obligatory attendance at morning worship, the remainder of the day was ours. We were free from the numerous money- earning jobs all poor children were obliged to undertake.

After an early lunch of bread and jam, about ten of us set off on our expedition, our route lying via a maze of lanes and tracks and over fields to the pools. Firstly we stopped at Marton Pool which was fairly close to the Hall. Next we went to nearby Fenemere Pool, which was somewhat larger, lying between the hamlets of Eyton and Fenemere. A chilly wind blew down upon us as it swept across the plain, and we were in constant sight of the Welsh mountains about 15 miles or so beyond us. The purpose of our excursion was to search for waterhen's eggs which could be found in the rushes and reeds near the water's edge. Gathering the eggs was no easy task, but could be achieved with long poles to which we tied old spoons. A great deal of patience was required as the eggs were tiny. The slightest jerk rendered an egg lost. Inevitably, one of us fell into the pool and emerged shaking and covered in duck-weed, having to remain in this state for the long trek home. Being country children, we never took all the eggs; if there were three in a nest, we took two – if five we took three. The tiny eggs were carried home with care, usually in a boy's cap and shared out equally when we reached the village. The eggs were always fried for our tea.

Those of us who were not soaked (or too cold) continued through the village to get more eggs at the small black pool on the roadside near Alderton, a short distance beyond Balderton Hall. This was more easily accessible and slightly closer to home.

A notable village landmark was 'The Rock', an exposed outcrop of grey rock stretching from near the top of Myddle Bank along the roadside, interspersed with golden gorse bushes. The initials and names of children of past generations were carved everywhere. Little foot-holes had been worn away by children climbing up, and little slides by children coming down. Boys wore the bottoms thin in their trousers, and girls their knickers. We also wore the toes out of our old shoes and received many warnings from our parents to keep away from the rock.

In those days village entertainment was practically non-existent apart from two concerts which I can recall at Myddlewood Reading Room. But nearby Harmer Hill Sunday School were quite adept at organising a spectacular show. Marjorie and I learnt from school friend, May of Webscott, of the imminence of such a concert, in which she would be taking part. Kindly Mrs Painter gave us each 1d for admission to the chapel. We set off early to ensure a favourable position in the gallery at the rear of the chapel from where we could be assured of a good view of the proceedings.

All evening we recognised our friend May as she appeared in different sketches. Then, all too soon, came the last act, which was May singing solo. Her mother had sewn a costume of a London Flower Girl and she carried a basket of fresh flowers. May sang 'Won't you buy my pretty flowers' (an old Victorian ballad). The chapel was very full, and the audience shouted, 'Sing it again.' So she obliged. Again the cry went up 'Sing it again.' May did so, but this time she threw the flowers from her basket into the audience.

Then to our utter astonishment, people began to throw pennies onto the roughly constructed platform. Some even threw half-crowns, which glistened in the lamp-light. Coins filled the stage, still May sang on, picking up the money and placing it in her basket, until she had cleared the area. We had never in our lives seen so much money. Then followed the applause, which was well deserved, for she had a delightful voice, and sang with a confidence not expected in a country girl of nine years.

When we had a few moments to spare (which was not often) Hopscotch was one of our favourite games. We played in the lane outside the cottage. Our young sister Elsie, while waiting for her turn, bounced on the drain-cover in the lane near our garden gate. To our horror she disappeared completely. We ran to the drain, which was full of dirty water, but there was no sign of our little sister.

It was around lunch time and we saw uncle Tom (Husbands) approaching on his bike, after a lunchtime drink at the *Red Lion*. (He was responsible for cutting drainage ditches on the lanes of the estate, which his father had done before him). We ran to him, talking at once and frantically related what had happened. He quickly got down on his knees and extricated Elsie by her hair. What emerged was not recognisable as our sister, but a black slimy figure covered in fifth and slugs. Tom carried her into the wash-house and we helped clean her down with newspaper and rhubarb leaves. Tom told Mother what had happened and water was hastily heated on the range in kettles and pans to bath Elsie.

She recovered remarkably quickly from this ordeal and no doctor was called to examine her. Mother put her to sit close to the fire with a cup of senna tea; this being the only cure she knew.

When harvesting at Houlston Farm, we children walked there, usually with my good friend Marjorie, in the hot summer sunshine, handkerchiefs tied round our heads with knots in the corners. We carried Father sandwiches and cold tea to the harvest field, so that he could work on until dark.

Whilst there, we enjoyed superb games of hide and seek in the golden fields, concealing ourselves behind the stooks, endeavouring not to squash pimpernels. Poppies and corn flowers sadly were lopped off by the giant reaper but the tiny scarlet pimpernel outwittingly survived.

A threshing machine was usually hired from Wem just for a day or two. The implement was drawn by a horse and used in the farmyard.

The machine beat out grain from the straw, which was a dusty operation. The grain then went to the mill and the straw provided fodder for horses and cattle on the farm.

On Sundays we gathered chestnuts and hazelnuts in season, in the woods, which we later roasted on the range. There were so many that we gave some away.

We often played with the children at Alford Farm (in the village centre – near the Inn). We tied a rope to a beam in the Dutch Barn to slide down – it was great fun!

Whilst there, we had the opportunity to use the closet, located in the pretty garden at the front of the farm, yet hidden from the road by bushes. What made this particular closet a little unusual, was that the wooden seat was very long, with three individual holes; a small one for the children, a larger one for the lady of the house, and an even bigger hole for the master. Each had a lid. The seat was scrubbed regularly, and the night-soil emptied often by farm workers.

CHAPTER THREE

The Great War

Like people of every town and village in Great Britain the population of Myddle was heavily involved in the 'war to end all wars' of 1914-1918 (World War I). There was enormous anti-German feeling at the time, and tens of thousands of men joined up. At first agricultural workers such as Father were encouraged to remain on the land because of the vital importance of food production. But as the war progressed and millions of lives were lost in futile battles to move the Belgian Front a few hundred yards, the Government was gradually forced to call up all able-bodied men who were not too old to fight, leaving women to take over many jobs including those of farm labourers.

Thus Father came to enlist for war service. He had never really been healthy but would not previously have seen a doctor to find out why. He was now discovered to suffer from bronchitis, sufficiently seriously to prevent him being enrolled for service overseas.

Instead, he was accepted as an army field cook with the Kings Shropshire Light Infantry, training at Shrewsbury Barracks, then being posted to camps at Oswestry and Barry.

With the huge numbers of men now in Army service, there were simply not enough buildings in which to house them all, so Father found himself, despite bronchitis, under canvas, like so many others. After two years or so, bronchitis had given way to pneumonia, and he was invalided out of Army service.

He returned home on a special train carrying sick and wounded soldiers to Baschurch station, Mother having to arrange for Mr Mullinux (the local carrier) to meet him there. An Army Nurse accompanied the sick soldiers and during the journey Father had shown her the pretty lace doilies made by soldiers at the camp, which he had purchased as a gift for his wife. His illness had prevented him leaving the camp to get Mother anything from the town.

The nurse took the little silver brooch she was wearing out of her coat and said, 'Take this, it will make a nice gift for your wife,' and gave it to Father who was overwhelmed by her kindness. The brooch remains in the family. Mother treasured it and wore it for many years until the pin broke; the anonymous nurse could not have known how much pleasure it would give to Mother, who had little jewellery. She wore it at the neck of a blouse – blouses and long skirts were the fashion in those days.

Mother had acquired another treasured possession while Father had been away on War service. She struggled to purchase a sewing machine by paying 2/6d per week for a heavy Singer model. She was always blissfully happy when operating the machine and could be heard either singing or whistling, as she fed stuff in to be stitched. (Life was very hard, especially for Mother, and there was little to sing about in those days). In common with other machine owners, she was now able to volunteer to make sandbags to help the war effort. The kits were delivered ready cut-out in strong calico, which she machined, leaving an end open. Before acquisition of the machine, all the sewing she did was by hand!

When Father had sufficiently recovered, he commenced work as a labourer on the estate farm, Houlston Manor. Later our friend Annie's father, Alfred, joined him at the same farm. This man had survived the Great War but, like so many others, would soon die from its delayed effects – he had been the victim of gas poisoning in France, which later developed into tuberculosis, and he only worked for a short time before he died.

Uncle Jack (Ebrey) Father's brother served in France and returned to Myddle on crutches.

One of Mother's brothers was taken prisoner in the conflict and died as a prisoner in Baghdad (Turkish Arab Lands) part of the Ottoman Empire at the time.

W. Husbands' name appears on the War Memorial (not a direct family member at this time but he was the brother of Tom Husbands, who married my Aunt Ethel).

I recall Mother taking me to a military funeral. The soldier, who had died in 1916, was Sergeant Saunders of Houlston, aged 39. I stood with Mother to watch the ceremony held near the old sundial on which steps we often played. The scene on this occasion was very sombre; a soldier fired a gun into the air and many military personnel were in attendance. A grey granite block, with a scroll engraved upon it, now marks the spot.

There was much sorrow in the village as news of dead servicemen filtered through to their loved ones and friends.

Not many women served in the Great War from this area. However, my Aunt Ethel (Father's sister) volunteered. She became an officer's Bat-woman in the Royal Flying Corps (the RAF was formed in April 1918 by amalgamating the Royal Flying Corps with the Royal Naval Air Service). For part of the war, aunt was stationed at Shawbury Airfield, the nearest to Myddle. We were all very proud of Aunt Ethel.

Upon cessation of hostilities, Ethel returned to her previous employment, where she was warmly welcomed back.

The entire school attended a special memorial service to the fallen of the parish at the end of the war. Firstly, a service was held inside the church, then we gathered, on a cold wintry morning, in the churchyard for the unveiling of the War Memorial. I stood near the mistress, Mrs Porch, who wept bitterly throughout the service, having lost a brother during the hostilities.

The stone cross stands at the top of three steps, near the

road to the left of the lych gate, and the names of 24 young men
who never returned to their beloved Shropshire are inscribed on
it:

J.C. Walford	Sgt. R.E.K. Lloyd	J.T. Thompson
J. Taylor	A.E. Saunders	H.O. Micklewright
E.P. Yeomans	J.C. Bebb	W. Husbands
J.H. Jones	S.C. Cooke	J.E. Downes
Lce.Cpl. H. Mullinux	A.E. Boliver	J. Eaton
Corpl. W. Reeves	A.W. Asterley	J. Jones
R.C. Lloyd	J. Garmston	Corpl F· Brown
Lce.Cpl. Whitfield	T. Ellis	P.W. Micklewright

Families and friends placed flowers and wreaths which were
banked high around the base of the cross.

In a small community like ours, everyone knew each of
the dead servicemen personally. These 24 dead men had all lived
within the parish, ie. the villages of Myddle, Harmer Hill and
surrounding hamlets, and like the vast number of men from
other parts of Britain [totalling 704,803], had never returned
after the war. In this way the Great War had been as terrible
a tragedy as elsewhere. Many others died afterwards from the
delayed effects of the horrendous battles in France and Flanders,
as a result of shell-shock, mustard gas or wounds.

Inside the church, a Roll of Honour was erected on the
south wall, in memory of men from the Parish who fell in the
Great War. On the same board (although this is a little unusual)
are the names of men who served under arms. Here father's and
his brother's names appear.

J. Ebrey
H. Ebrey

A festival of peace was celebrated in most villages at the
cessation of hostilities and ours was no exception. A marquee

was erected in the school playing-field and women helped with cakes and sandwiches; races were organised for the children, with small prizes. Men were set the task of catching a pig, which was let loose in the next field so as not to upset the stalls. A presentation was made to the children of a commemorative peace mug and sweets. Grinshill Band played at one end of the tent, the most beautiful tunes I, as a small child, had ever heard; many were from the war. Later the marquee was cleared of tables and chairs, and adults and young people danced the evening away, some overspilling into the field which was lit with lanterns.

This was one of the few occasions in our childhood for which we were made new frocks by Mother, and that is probably why I recall them. They were of white cotton trimmed with lace. Mother had put insertion lace at the waist and threaded this with red, white and blue ribbons!

I have previously mentioned that Father's brother, my uncle Jack, was invalided out of the Great War and returned home to Myddle on crutches. Having been posted overseas he had travelled further than other members of my family and consequently he had a broader outlook on life. He set his sights on becoming a smallholder, rather than returning to farm labour. I believe a Resettlement Grant was available due to his injuries and he firstly rented a smallholding, his children (a son and two daughters) largely helping him to run it. Much later he purchased his own smallholding at Emstrey, near Atcham.

Uncle possessed a certain business acumen, which was a little rare in our family. He seemed well-informed about local matters and heard, in advance, of plans to erect a new bridge at Atcham. It occurred to him that cart-horses would be required by the contractors in the construction of the bridge. He may have been taking a risk, but he purchased two horses at the next sale in Shrewsbury and, in due course, an advertisement appeared in the local newspaper inviting owners to tender their stock. Uncle's horses were offered, accepted, and they conveyed heavy carts laden with building materials to the site, for which he was well paid. During the summer months the horses were left to graze in the water meadows, but during the winter uncle was responsible for feeding them.

He was a most enterprising man and his smallholding was very successful.

Jack's son Harold, my cousin, was a keen horseman. He rode whenever the opportunity arose. One year he gained first-place in a jumping event at Shrewsbury Show. He later went on to open a successful riding school of his own near Shrewsbury.

Modern Myddle: the pump (foreground), the old school (now the village hall) and the pub, The Red Lion, in the background.

CHAPTER FOUR

A Rather Scant Education

Mr Porch was Headmaster of the Church of England village school in the early 1900s, the same school where Richard Gough the famous local historian, born in 1635, had received his earliest education.

Our Headmaster was also a watercolour artist with imaginative insight. [Two views of the interior of St Peter's Church, painted by Mr Percy Porch over 50 years ago, were discovered and displayed at an exhibition in June 1987 at the new Rectory.] He considered that his pupils might be talented in this way, if given the opportunity and materials with which to paint and express themselves. Paints were not provided in village schools then and art had no place in the curriculum. Mr and Mrs Porch (his wife was also a teacher at Myddle school) actively attempted to remedy this situation. They decided to hold a sale of children's work to raise funds. With limited finances, they purchased materials and wools for the girls in Mrs Porch's sewing class to make saleable articles, such as knitted jumpers for small children, little socks (Mrs Porch helping to turn the heels), knickers, petticoats, work-bags, fringed mats to stand oil lamps on, etc, etc – in fact anything which might sell.

The Headmaster had then to overcome the School Governors' rather circumspect view on such a radical step. He sought a meeting with them, and eventually they gave permission for a sale of children's work. This event was unique to the school and when the day of the sale arrived, Mr Porch seized the opportunity to bring his framed paintings from home. These included scenes painted in Devonshire as well as local beauty spots. There were studies of rhododendrons painted in the Rectory garden and scenes of the church and village. The paintings were displayed on the walls of the classrooms for all to see.

The sale was opened by the elegant Marchioness of Cambridge (of Shotton Hall). The children elected Maggie Fernell, one of the farmer's daughters who was neatly dressed at all times, to present her Ladyship with a bouquet of flowers upon arrival.

The Marchioness was well impressed by the paintings and the scheme generally, and she agreed to give financial aid to the project. With this, and the money raised by the sale, pallets, tubes of watercolours, paint brushes and paper were purchased. This was how art classes began at Myddle School in the 1920s. We sketched and painted mainly in the Lower Road area, where an abundance of wild flowers was always to be found. We had gathered flowers here for Mother many times, but had never examined them carefully.

Now under Mr Porch's skilful guidance we discovered for the first time the depths and intensity of colours. We explored and mixed the many shades of purples, pinks and reds of rhododendrons; the soft delicate greens of the new ferns and the reds and pinks of campions. The perfect petal formations of rosebay willowherbs, foxgloves and bluebells, in their seasons, were studied in detail. At other times our heavy wooden forms were moved into the playground and we concentrated our attention on the shades and textures of the solid sandstone buildings nearby. Another location chosen for the study of prickly yellow gorse shrubs, was the old quarry. My painting this day was one of those selected by Mr Porch for display on the classroom wall.

Whilst many of my contemporaries will remember the canings inflicted upon us by Mr Porch with horror, as indeed

I do; the artistic skills which had been lying dormant in many of us until awakened by him, were to stand me in good stead all my life. Certainly I shall always be grateful to his memory for the lessons on colours and textures, and the opportunity he gave us to produce work of imagination and creativity which, in my case, extended into dress designing and sewing skills, which have remained my greatest delights.

The school was at the centre of the village, adjoining the inn. (It is reassuring today that the old school has been tastefully preserved as a village hall, particularly in view of its past connections with Richard Gough).

There were two other teachers, Mrs Porch (whom I have already referred to) and Miss Ellen Cank, who cycled each day from Harmer Hill, where in later life at the age of 68 (as Mrs Sutton) she was one of the victims in a tragic triple murder. The school had nearly 100 pupils, with ages ranging from 5 to 14 years in three classes.

Slates were all that children in the first class had to write on – later we progressed to actual paper with pens and ink!

The Headmaster's gaunt red brick Victorian house stood uncomfortably close to our cottage, at the foot of Myddle Bank on the south side. A few holly bushes occupied the garden.

Mr Porch was the first in the locality to purchase a wireless (radio). Anxious that we should learn about broadcasting, and how sounds travelled through the air, we were taken into his home, six at a time, during the afternoon of a transmission. A high pole in the garden carried a wire which entered the house. We took it in turns to wear the two sets of ear-phones, through which we could clearly hear people talking. Later, at school, we were required to write an essay about the new experience.

The next member of the community to purchase a set was Mr Latham, a tradesman, who lived in an attractive black and white cottage at Myddlewood. He soon began to manufacture small wireless sets himself, for sale, and the batteries were taken back to his workshop for re-charging. Father purchased one about three years later from Mr Latham and we always referred to it as 'the listening in' which is, of course, what one did. This innovation was the beginning of the end to the isolation of rural life.

White calico aprons, with frills on the shoulders, and fastening with tapes at the back of the neck and at the waist, were worn by girls for school. Mother made all ours. The frills were ironed with a special gauffer iron, which was rather like a long pair of scissors with round blades. These exceptionally pretty aprons covered any old frock that we might be wearing beneath. Immediately upon return from school they were removed and hung away in the bedroom until next day, Mother was very strict about this. She also made our 'liberty bodices' of white flannel, which she quilted for warmth; also our flannel petticoats.

Mother walked a 10-mile round trip to obtain the cotton materials for frocks and pinafores at 6d per yard. During the school holidays, we immensely enjoyed these walks with her; the 5 miles to Bowens at Wem and the 5 miles back. We ran ahead and sat on the milestones while she caught up. A bottle of water was placed in the bottom of the pram for us all to share; there was always a baby in the family.

And registering the babies' births involved us in very long walks on the muddy, unsurfaced lanes. The Registrar was Miss Miles, who lived at the remote hamlet of Eyton, 2½ miles away, beyond Fenemere Pool (on a back lane to Baschurch). In those days a new baby was taken along and seen by the Registrar, even if it meant a 5 mile round trip for a mother who had recently given birth. When Dorothy was registered, I accompanied Mother, and we took it in turns to push the old pram.

After the birth of a new baby, the Rector, or a representative from the church, called at the cottage to make arrangements for Mother to attend a short service of thanksgiving after child-birth (the Churching of women). Attendance at this service was usually the first time Mother went out of doors after delivery.

Mother made pretty cotton gowns for all the babies,

threading ribbon through soft lace insertions. She helped others out too, being one of the few women to possess a sewing machine. The gowns were brought to her, cut out and tacked in readiness for machining. Emma Wright gave her odd pieces of narrow ribbon.

Babies in those days wore long cream flannel petticoats which folded at the bottom and tied with tapes; these were worn from about six weeks. The gowns, which were much longer, were worn on top. A small 'head shawl' was used to cover the baby's head and shoulders.

Pieces of open weave flannel were wound around the baby's stomach; this was to cover the sore navel, and support the baby when it cried. The flannel, purchased by the yard and cut into long strips to avoid uncomfortable seams, was wrapped around the baby several times, then stitched in place with a bodkin and thread. This was done every day and called swaddling.

But to return to my schooldays: whenever we had a baby in the house, I had to stay home from school to help Mother if she was in bed or otherwise unable to cope (or had to walk to the Registrar at Eyton). This was just accepted as normal in large families.

At least I was unlikely to catch ringworm when I was off school. Farmers' children spasmodically attended school with patches of ringworm in their hair, which they had picked up from their animals. This skin disease was easily transmitted to other children, although caps were worn to try and prevent the spread. The only cure seemed to be to paint the affected patches with iodine.

The distinguished-sounding 'Church Girls Friendly Society', was merely a group of girls from school who were capable of fine hand sewing. I must admit that I was privileged to be among their number. Each month we were allowed to leave school early and walk as a party to the Rectory to pursue our sewing techniques. After the statutory curtsy to the rector's wife seated at the head of their superbly-polished oak dining table, we joined her. Sessions were always preceded by a short prayer. At each place lay an embroidered work-bag of white calico, containing the article of sewing which we were making. It might be knickers, petticoats, nightdresses, etc.

Everything had to be neatly and strongly hand-sewn, with lace inserts, as directed by Mrs Woolward. Her housekeeper ironed transfers on some of the garments, where appropriate, and we embroidered the designs using silk. Sadly, we only completed a short strip on each occasion; this was due to the obligatory exercise around the neat lawned gardens we were required to take, before being summoned back to the Rectory, by bell, for tea and cakes. We dispersed after prayers. When eventually the articles were completed, they were passed for the sale-of-work organised by the church to provide funds to help the poor of the parish. The 'Society' was an interesting diversion from school lessons, to which we looked forward with eager anticipation.

Of course we had sewing lessons at school with Mrs Porch, and much emphasis was placed upon needlework then, before sewing machines became commonplace. The boys meanwhile were dispatched to keep the Headmaster's garden tidy, under the guise of gardening lessons! One particular year the village was plagued with rats. In an effort to help stem the outbreak, Mr Porch offered to pay 2d per rat's tail, for any taken to school by the boys. They accordingly set traps and many were caught. He disposed of the tails by burying them in his garden. The conscientious lads digging next day, found the tails which the Headmaster had buried. These were quickly cleaned, concealed in their pockets, and presented again at school when an unsuspecting Mr Porch, full of praise and approbation for the boys' splendid endeavours, paid up once more! It was rare indeed for village boys to get the better of the judicious Mr Porch!

The pupils included a young crippled boy, who wore calipers, and lived at a farm some two miles distant from the village. He was transported to school by pony and trap, his elder brother driving it. This little trap, almost circular in shape, was made of wood, with seats all round. The reins rested on a polished brass bar fixed across the front. Doris' mother permitted the horse to graze all day in her field in the Lower Road.

Our little friend Annie was born at Newton-on-the-Hill, and later her family moved into the cottage which we had vacated at Balderton. The two brothers picked Annie up from her cottage gate, and she rode with them on two wheels, chariot style, to school and home again afterwards. Children from the age of about six years were allowed to drive these little traps along the unsurfaced lanes, unaccompanied. I am not aware of a single accident.

Mr Porch was characteristically irritated the day he discovered that not one of us had heard of the North Shropshire plain. To correct our lapse of knowledge we were marched en bloc to Myddle Hill to a location near the stile. Here he pointed north-east with his cane, to the gentle rolling flat plain which lay ahead and explained that this was the plain of North Shropshire. This was a breathtakingly beautiful view at any season of the year, but especially in mid-summer, when the patchwork of fields was predominantly golden-yellow. The flat rural landscape stretched for many miles, as far as the eye could see, and he explained that remarkable cloud formations could be observed across the plain. Turning westwards, he led us to a position where field boundaries could just be discerned on the foothills of the Berwyn Mountains. This was one of the best geography lessons we ever had!

Caning took place all too frequently and was brutal, always severely across the hands with a bamboo cane, boys and girls with no discrimination. The wrong answers in arithmetic or boys answering back usually provoked a caning, as did absenteeism or lateness. The children of smallholders were required to help their parents by taking churns of milk to catch the train, driving the pony and trap themselves to Baschurch, and consequently being late for school. In the case of poor families, such as ours, the eldest child was kept at home to look after the other children if Mother was ill. One particular family were frequently late or absent because they simply had no bread for their mid-day lunch. Bread was only delivered once a week, and they either had to go without lunch or have the morning off school to walk to Baschurch for a loaf. We were caned whether we took a note from our parents explaining our absence or not!

The youngest brother of one of my school friends was caned severely and regularly because he was left-handed, and was a little short-sighted too. Because of the repeated victimisation of this little boy, his parents took him away from the school and sent him to a private school in Shrewsbury.

Each year my parents were at odds with Mr Porch over damson picking. We possessed numerous productive trees which lined the long garden and there were fertile trees on our top field. These damsons were a crucial source of income for my poor parents, but the fruit had to be picked. I was usually the one retained at home to look after the baby and help Mother with the harvesting.

One particular skirmish with Mr Porch involved us all. My sisters Emily and Elsie went to school as usual. During the course of the morning, Emily was sent home with a note, asking why I was not at school. Mother then kept Emily at home too, and ignored the note, glad to have another pair of hands.

Next it was Elsie's turn to arrive on the doorstep with another letter, this time requesting that Emily and I be sent to school immediately. Needless to say Mother ignored this note also. Mr Porch then dispatched a farmer's son with a note for Mother, demanding that she send Elsie, Emily and me to school directly. Mother hardly dare set him picking our damsons too, so while he waited, she took out the rarely-used ink and pen from the dresser and on the back of the latest communication wrote, in her singularly impressive handwriting, 'Thank you for sending my children home, I shall now get the damsons harvested in no time. The threat of school inspectors will not alarm me, I have a clear conscience – you sent the children home!'

But the row didn't end there; dogmatic Mr Porch felt it his duty to see Father in the evening, while we were all out in the garden. Voices were raised as we proceeded non-stop, gathering the small black fruit, and the threat of school inspectors was directed at Father. But they never called. We filled hessian sacks and carried them to Marton Corner where the damson agent for the village lived. The fruit had to be picked quickly, before the price fell. Much later a fruit dealer came to the village collecting, and Father was paid about three shillings per hamper; the price then dropped substantially as more and more damsons became available.

I have related that my parents were too poor ever to call a doctor out to us children, even when Elsie swallowed a quantity of foul drain water. A district nurse called occasionally at school, however, to inspect heads and children were given a note if they were not clean. This was regarded as the ultimate disgrace, and news of the recipients of such notes quickly spread through the village. A doctor called rarely at school to examine us, and a dentist didn't come until we were quite old and almost ready to leave. He filled one of my front teeth, using a drill which he operated with his foot, and the process was extremely painful. This took place in a redundant classroom. (I had my first toothbrush when I was 19). If our teeth became discoloured, we rubbed them with common salt, then spitting it out, and this cleaned any stains quite well.

The village pump, situated by the school playground, also served all the school's water needs. During spells of hot weather, when the water level dropped dramatically so that users had to pump for much longer than normal to draw water, Mrs Porch felt that schoolchildren might waste the precious commodity when drawing it for their lunch-time drink. It was her idea to fill a large bucket and take it into the classroom, where we queued as she sparingly doled out water, all drinking from the same cup!

The closets were near the main building; girls foremost, then boys behind, sharing the same roof. The teachers had the first in the row, which we were not allowed to enter under any circumstances. The latrine itself was a large brick container, under the wooden seat, which was emptied by hand with large ladles usually during the school holidays. The stench was quite revolting and pervaded the village; local men were paid 1/6d each for this task which was an appalling job.

One Christmas we watched from our window as Mr and Mrs Porch loaded cane baskets onto Mr Mullinux's dray, in preparation for the first stage of their seasonal visit to relatives in Bristol. Just prior to being driven to the station, Mrs Porch gave Mother a parcel of coloured ribbons and little handkerchiefs to wrap up for us, as she knew only too well that we would not be the recipients of any gifts. This was a kindly act for which we would always remember her.

But discipline at school, as at home, was very strict. If an adult entered the classroom to speak to a teacher (it might be the Rector, a school Governor, etc) we all had to stand and say 'Good morning, Sir,' and rise again when they left. Children were regularly given a good shaking for bad performance in lessons. I could not read very well, and can remember going home with bruises and finger marks on my arms, where Mrs Porch had held me tightly whilst shaking me violently. On another occasion Mrs Porch was about to hit Emily, I spoke out and begged her not to, saying that Emily's nose would be sure to bleed if she hit her, so she hit me instead, for being so rude and outspoken. That's how it was then.

I always felt that I never really learnt a lot at school, one way or another. Besides I missed school so often – what with picking damsons, looking after the younger children, and helping Mother in all sorts of ways – that I was rarely actually in school for a full week at a time.

CHAPTER FIVE

The Village Fiddler & Rare Parties

The simple Sunday School outing was a delight to the many under-privileged children in the village. It actually took place on a Sunday in those days. Grinshill Hill, a local beauty spot, was the destination (four miles from Myddle).

Mrs Griffiths, our Sunday School teacher, borrowed a flat dray and wagon horse from their farm and drove this herself along the quiet green lanes. A wide-brimmed straw hat shaded her eyes from the sun. After games and sandwiches at Clive, we climbed the gullet path at the side of the church, following this through woods to the summit (630ft above sea level). From here we could see the Shropshire landscape stretching out below us. Mrs Griffiths pointed out well-known landmarks naming churches, hamlets, villages and the famous landmass near Wellington – the Wrekin (1334ft). Wenlock Edge was visible, as were the Clee Hills, Longmynd near Church Stretton, the Stiperstones, the Long Mountain near Montgomery, the Berwyns (this was the range closest to our village), Peckforton Hill in Cheshire, sometimes (on a really clear day) we were told that even Cader Idris on the Welsh Coast was visible. I should add that Mrs Griffiths had been a schoolteacher before her marriage and was well qualified to organise our outing. The only place in Shropshire we really knew well was our own village and it was a great thrill for us to observe the sheer size of the area round us.

Another year the fish cart, with low sides, was kindly lent by the Furnells at Alford farm who also provided their wagoner to

A 1930s photo of Helen Ebrey at Myddle Rock, where village children played over the centuries.

drive it to Grinshill. Three school benches were placed inside for the children and a larger party was transported on this occasion. Mr & Mrs Porch, who were also Sunday School teachers, followed behind on their bikes.

Christmas at home was scarcely different from any other day; we ate a little better than usual, that was all, as Father would have slaughtered one of our cockerels.

We had the Christmas Party for farmworkers' children to look forward to, held at Houlston Manor while Father was employed there. Mother even knitted us each a new frock for this special occasion. They were practical warm woollen ones, knitted in a lacy pattern in dark wool; a quick wipe over our old shoes with a damp rag to remove any traces of cow dung, and we were in high spirits for this convivial affair.

Each Christmas we were given permission by Father to go carol-singing with a few friends, and generally set off in the Myddlewood direction. The cottages gave the appearance of being snug and warm inside, with gleaming brass oil lamps burning on tables and sills, and the bright effect of warm colours reflected from log fires. The occupants were so comfortable inside, they refused to open their doors to let in the cold night-air. Although we sang and knocked, no money was ever earned carol singing. This was really of no consequence, we were more than rewarded by the sheer joy of being out of doors together on a wintry evening in bright moonlight, after bedtime. Our singing alas, was a complete disaster!

During severe winters, of which we had more than our fair share in this part of North Shropshire, the running brook became frozen. Many folk braved the cold to watch children slipping and sliding on the moonlight-sparkling ice. Moonlight was, of course, an important factor in the village before electric lighting came.

Christmas was not the only season when we enjoyed ourselves. Unpredictable events could, and did, happen to liven things up in the village.

There was great excitement one evening when news spread that a bi-plane had crash-landed in Fenemere Lane. As far as I can recall the year would be about 1920. It was very nearly dark when we set off with Mother, taking the hurricane-lamp, to see the crashed plane for ourselves. There were many people in the lane, all talking excitedly, and hurrying in the same direction. When we arrived we saw an immense object, resting on the hedge bank, and lying right across the lane. The pilot, thankfully, was not dead, the first on the scene having helped him out. We were amazed by its great size. Our inspection was curtailed somewhat by encroaching darkness, but the beams from the many lanterns now at the site revealed the large propeller, immense double wings and relatively small take-off/landing wheels.

We chatted to the village children who were there and to many others who had reached the spot from distant hamlets in the opposite direction. We took bits and pieces from the damaged aircraft to keep as momentos. Marjorie had a piece of the propeller and her brothers took pieces of the fuselage. The plane was a complete write-off and was removed in sections by cart next day. Some of us agreed that it might be a good idea to return in daylight, immediately after school, which we did, but not a trace of the aircraft could be found; damaged hedges were the only evidence that it had ever crashed. It was generally assumed that the aircraft had been flying from Shawbury, this being the nearest airfield.

There were the bare-back donkey rides which I shared with school-friend Reta, a farmer's daughter from Webscott. She was sent to Myddle to collect provisions from the store. On the way home, Reta often offered me a ride; the donkey trotting along the Lower Road and back to the farm.

Myddle fête, held in the Rectory garden, was a great crowd-puller. Colourful bunting and flags suspended from trees in the garden and across the lane, added a certain festive importance to this annual event. Grinshill bandsmen, in their neat braided uniforms, played well-known tunes and marches which penetrated the cottages of older inhabitants, unable due to infirmity to attend the event themselves.

Races were organised for children, teas provided, and we were allowed to ramble at leisure through the woods at the rear of the Rectory. A lady from Harmer Hill had her usual stall where home-made toffee could be purchased, and it was, in quantity. The farmers' wives provided second-hand shoes and clothes, and village wives crowded around this stall, indeed it was from here that most of our wear originated. The Rector owned several vintage coaches, which were never brought out on display, but which the boys could view by peering in through cracks in the doors of the coach-houses at the side of this noble house. I may have already mentioned Miss Emma Wright and her favourite pastime which was delicate Victorian embroidery, always worked solely in white cotton or silk, on white fabric. She regularly had a stall where her beautiful pieces (knickers, petticoats, chemises, nightdresses, blouses, etc) could be purchased; generously donating all proceeds to the fête. Later, dancing took place on the lawn, and a concert was organised with poetry readings and singing by a group of farmers. The entire village participated, one way or another, and the fête was an experience of pleasure.

Ice cream first came to Myddle via an old motor-bike and odd-shaped sidecar. The 'salesman' provided no wafers or biscuits or any type of container, we were asked to fetch a cup from home, which he filled for a penny. Public health legislation was practically non-existent then!

The annual Shrewsbury Show was an event outside most people's pockets. Nevertheless we enjoyed it, although at no time had we the good fortune to attend. I joined other children who congregated on Myddle Hill to watch the unusually heavy flow of traffic into Shrewsbury. There were special charabanc excursions from Wrexham, Overton, Ellesmere and Chester. We watched early cars, like our doctor's, which were a rare sight in the village. Many ponies-and-traps joined the great cavalcade. All this happened early in the morning, before school.

In the evening we took bottles of water from the pump and sat on the grass verge to watch the cavalcade return. Trippers in open-topped charabancs, who had consumed a drink or two, threw pennies to us as we waved. (Some even threw rock and humbugs, which they had bought at the show). As I have already said, at the time few ordinary village folk had the means of attending the Show, even though it took place only eight miles away. However, everyone enjoyed the grand firework display on the last evening, which could be viewed from a particular field on the Harmer Hill Road.

Fortuitously the show occurred after harvest, and the farmer who rented this field was happy to let villagers converge upon it for this annual event, which was quite spectacular and could be seen clearly in the night sky eight miles to the south. The first show had taken place in 1874. Unfortunately the wind at no time carried the hot air balloons from the show in the direction of Myddle!

The custodians of our magnificent seventeenth century inn, which dominated the village centre, were Mr & Mrs Colemere. We were told by our little friend Annie, that when her mother Sarah left Myddle School, she was employed by the Colemeres as what was in those days known as a 'nurse girl' to their baby son Harold.

Much land was then appended to the inn, several fields in the village as well as fields at Myddlewood. Mrs Colemere was a good friend to my Mother, and at harvest time I helped her by taking a sandwich tea to the men hired for hay-making in their fields at Myddlewood. I did this for two or three days, after school, until work was complete, enabling them to work until it grew dark.

Mother made Mrs Colemere's neat white aprons, which were long and covered an even longer black dress. This was how the two became friends. From a leather belt around her waist was usually suspended a bunch of heavy keys.

The Colemeres were a musically talented family, which was quite a rare attribute in those days. On Sabbath afternoons Mr Colemere fiddled for the entertainment and pure delight of musically-deprived children. We all fell into this category, the only music we heard being the church organ. (The old harmonium which pined sadly in the schoolroom was used rarely, and then only as a means of providing the correct leading note for older girls when singing hymns).

The inn's lattice parlour windows, over the tiny street garden, were flung open and our village fiddler (Mr Colemere) began an impromptu concert. At his invitation, which hung on the first magic notes to pervade the Sunday silence, children tumbled from their cottage doors and hurried to the inn. There outside the open window, we watched as if bewitched as Mr Colemere's nimble fingers bowed and plucked, his agility producing a musical feast for his appreciative young listeners, as he performed lively jigs and simple reels from memory. This was a special Sunday treat for us all.

Meanwhile, Harold, their only son, could now play the piano proficiently. Someone had the idea that if a piano could be hoisted into the club room over the stables, the potential existed for weekly dances. This initiative was implemented and well patronised among young people. The charge for admission was set at sixpence, but Mrs Colemere always allowed children in

Helen pictured three days before
her 20th birthday.
In Birmingham, Helen at last had a
kindly employer. Although she had
to share an attic bedroom (with
skylight window) with another maid,
Helen was well-regarded
and happy.

free of charge, and sent us all off at 10pm. Some time later, due to
the success of this initial venture, Harold hired a drummer, and
eventually other instrumentalists joined them, and their quality
and performance improved significantly. Indeed, they became
known locally as the 'Colemere Band' and were booked to play
at village dances, weddings, fêtes and so on. One Harold Wells
of Baschurch ferried the band and their instruments around to
venues in his ancient taxi. This venture put Myddle on the map!

We looked forward to the weekly hops, as not a great deal
happened in the village during the evening, and they diverted
our attention from the daily grind. We dressed in any old frock
which might be clean. Elsie, however, begged Mother for a new
dress specially for the dances, but Mother said no! We discussed
this request as we sat round at the next dance when Marjorie's
sister offered to run a frock up for Elsie, charging her only for the
stuff. She said Elsie could pay back gradually, as and when able to
earn a little money unknown to our parents.

The clandestine dance gown thus took shape. It was red in
colour and ankle-length as was then fashionable. It complemented

Elsie's raven-black hair and good looks, and she was never short
of partners. This precious garment was kept at Marjorie's home
for safety, and she brought it to the hops neatly folded in a brown
paper bag each time, Elsie changing in the dressing room.
We were a little fearful of word reaching our parents of Elsie's
spectacular appearances, but thankfully it never did.

When the bar closed and Mrs Colemere had a few minutes
to spare, she made an urn of tea which the men carried up to
the clubroom for her, providing us all with a free cup before our
departure.

The interior of the inn was, by virtue of its age, quite
charming. It possessed an abundance of exposed beams, low
ceilings, gleaming brass and copper and highly-polished antique
oak furniture. The ever-present smell of furniture polish lingered
in the old rooms.

There were five bedrooms, one private room over the lounge
which was the innkeeper's, and four guest rooms, although the
Colemeres did not seek this type of clientele. A subsequent
owner, Mrs Lloyd, who had commenced taking guests, showed
me around during a visit to my parents some years later. She had
acquired a full-size knight in glistening armour who was placed
on a landing! The guest rooms were nicely furnished with double
beds and white cotton honeycomb bedspreads lay on top. There
were marble-topped wash stands, housing a pretty jug and bowl
and little porcelain matching soap dish. A wooden towel rail was
positioned close-by. (Mains water had not yet reached Myddle.)

An unusual feature was the lack of privacy, in that visitors
were obliged to walk through one another's bedrooms. This
arrangement was fairly common in the village, and most cottage
bedrooms were approached via other bedrooms. Our dwelling
was a little unusual in this respect, in that the living-room stairs
led to a long narrow landing, from which individual access-
doors to the two bedrooms was gained.

CHAPTER SIX

Poaching

Illegal poaching was a commonplace occurrence in the days of large families and low incomes. Father encroached in this way not under cover of darkness, but by the half-light of dawn. He slung his double-barrelled shotgun carefully around his neck, under his coat. This was a trick of his brother-in-law (Jack Grice); hands then hung free, and the gun was not easily detected. Mother had stitched extra big 'poaching pockets' on the inside of his old coat to conceal his booty. He shot, or set traps, in the screen of the coppices, on land near where he was employed at Houlston. The area was susceptible to flooding and an obvious habitat for wild duck in the numerous naturally-formed ponds near the Manor. His employer had no objection, but pheasants were game birds, the shooting of which, or even disturbance of their eggs, was forbidden.

Traps were also set in our own orchard, where Father sprinkled Indian corn and other tasty inducements. This was how we rarely enjoyed the luxury of rabbit or wild duck.

There were gamekeepers on the estate and a policeman stationed at Harmer Hill, but fortunately for us Father was never caught, either shooting or setting traps. Nor can I ever recall anyone being brought before the bench for poaching in the parish when I was young.

I had to clean Father's double barrel shot gun weekly, which stood in the corner of the living room.

After Mother had skinned a rabbit, and we had one fairly often when Father went poaching, she hung the skin in the wash house. A woman called every week, all around the village and paid 6d or 9d for each skin. She took them away, cured them and they were sold to furriers.

The only problem with living in the centre of the village, was that everyone knew when Father had been poaching because of the glorious smell emitting from our living room. The door had to remain open because of the intense heat from the range. Mother's speciality was cooking rabbit, which she roasted with herbs, but she was a good cook generally and had the happy knack of making something special out of nothing!

CHAPTER SEVEN

The Village Pump

Our only source of drinking water was the village pump, located in a small area walled off from the school playground. In winter, although lagged with straw, it inevitably became frozen; then villagers would hurry to the iron pump with hot cinders or boiling water, in an attempt to unfreeze it. All our drinking water had to be carried to the cottage, where it was stored in the cool pantry in a large glazed earthenware vessel which we called a stein.

The pump could reasonably be described as the hub of the village, for geographically speaking it was situated at the very centre. It was here that daily news and, dare I say, gossip, was gathered and passed on, while folk waited their turn patiently as buckets were first swilled, and then filled. The obtaining of drinking water was very much a village sound, buckets swinging lightly on the journey to the well, but weighing heavily on the carrier on the return route.

We considered ourselves fortunate in Myddle in having a conventional hand pump, as the inhabitants of nearby Harmer Hill experienced a more complicated procedure, in that their water was wound up frequently from a deep well. This was done by a donkey walking round in circles, supervised by a workman. At the time, postcards were available locally depicting a horse drawing up water, because this method was practically unique in the area. (The horse succeeded the donkey). When the donkey had raised the water to fill an underground tank, the inhabitants

Until 1960, the village pump next to the old school building was the centre of village life.

then operated a hand pump in the usual way, until the tank became dry again and the process was repeated. This method was necessitated by the significant height of Harmer Hill in relation to surrounding plains: the water-table here in Harmer Hill being much lower.

For washing purposes, rainwater was collected from the roof of our wash-house in huge butts. During periods of prolonged dry weather, getting on my knees, I scooped water from the brook which ran between the inn yard and the store, in a flat bowl-dish for mother's washing.

Another drinking-water well, with an old wooden pump, was situated at Myddlewood, opposite the cottage where the rector's coachman lived. It lay on the north of the lane, large sandstone slabs having been provided to step upon, and a high sandstone sink stood under the pump to accommodate buckets.

A third quaint little well could be found opposite the church, set neatly behind a sandstone wall, and not easily visible to a passing stranger. This mattered not as the water here was not sufficiently pure to drink, but was much used by visitors to the church for flowers. So neat was the construction of this well and its surrounds, that I suspect long before my life commenced it had been used as a source of drinking water. This was an open well, with no pump, and vessels had to be lowered into the water.

Three tiny well-worn steps, with stile, led into the churchyard corner across the road. A customary occupation of many folk in those days, especially on Sunday afternoons, was a leisurely stroll to the peaceful churchyard with flowers for the grave of a loved-one.

A regular user of this well was Mrs Shingler who occupied a smallholding near the top of the Gullet. Hers was the oldest remaining building in the Gullet, commanding remarkable views over the village and across to the church and castle. Daily Mrs Shingler drove her cattle through the village, the large beasts struggling awkwardly down the Gullet's steep uneven path, before bustling out, at a trot, onto the Bank bottom. Hers was not an easy task as she escorted the animals single-handed through the village. In dry weather a stop was made at the church well to water the cattle by means of a bucket, which she kept concealed beneath vegetation near the well, before continuing in the direction of the mountains to her pasture. (When eventually she sold her cattle, Mrs Shingler took over as village postwoman, upon Mr Wright's retirement).

Many occupants of outlying cottages used a yoke to support two buckets of water. These were generally made of elm, and had the advantage that water was carried away from the body, so clothes were less likely to become soaked when water slopped over the sides. It was very hard work nonetheless and had to be done frequently, in all weathers and in all states of health.

The considerable distance from Myddle of Aunt Ethel Husband's cottage seemed not to concern her greatly (maybe her forces' resolve). Every drop of drinking water had to be carried in a bucket from the village – some 1¼ miles in each direction. She usually biked in, and balanced the full bucket on the handlebar to walk home, water cascading over the sides as she pushed the cycle up the bank. She did this regularly for the best part of 15 years. During the winter she wore her old forces' trench-coat, long woollen skirt and heavy service shoes. Eventually, a kindly farmer with land near Ethel's cottage was allowed piped water

After a disastrous collapse in 1976, this was all that remained of the last standing wall of 12th century Myddle Castle.

to a nearby field for cattle, and he kindly let her draw from this supply. I daresay she missed her vocal encounters with folk on the way to the village well!

Merrington Well was something rather unusual by reason of the inscription on a large tablet secured in its decorative sandstone wall. We used to pass this well on our way to Merrington Green. It was used by gypsies at the Merrington encampment, being the closest for drinking water, although water for other purposes was available from various ponds on the heathland.

Piped water did not reach the village until well into the postwar years. Indeed the well in Myddle continued in use through the 1950s.

CHAPTER EIGHT

The Oddfellows Club
& the Ellesmere Workhouse

PIMHILL ODDFELLOWS CLUB

No working person could afford not to be a member of one of
the benevolent societies which existed at that time. Father paid
a few shillings every month into the Pimhill Oddfellows Club
(Harmer Hill Branch), and when Emily and I commenced work
at the farm, he had to pay for us as well, as our parents had all
our earnings. In times of illness, a claimant would receive five
shillings per week from the fund. The great bulk of the population
were farm labourers, and there was no form of sickness benefit in
those days, before the welfare state.

Uncle Jack Grice was Honorary Secretary. He collected
subscriptions, and brought round payments when needed,
which had to be properly signed for. In consequence he had the
unenviable task of reporting on any members claiming benefit,
who were observed out of doors at night after 9pm. There was
a rule of membership that claimants kept to a strict curfew. He
popped his head round the door at whist drives, pubs, dances,
etc to make sure claimants were not present after 9pm. It was
considered by the society that if a claimant had the zest to attend
such functions, he was fit enough to work.

Members used an upper room at the Bridgewater Arms, Harmer Hill (named after the Earl of Bridgewater, a distant owner of the Manor of Myddle), for meetings, games of billiards, dominoes, etc. Any curfew breakers were summoned to appear before a tribunal at one of these gatherings. Normally only a note from a doctor could excuse anyone, such was the seriousness of this offence.

The Oddfellows annual sports day was held in a field beside the pub. Giant carved swing-boats were the main attraction, hired specially for the occasion, and a varied programme of events was organised during the afternoon. The sports day was preceded by a church service, and the procession then made its way to the Bridgewater Arms led by Uncle Jack, dressed in his best Sunday suit and wearing an elaborately embroidered satin sash bearing the words 'Pimhill Oddfellows – Harmer Hill Branch.'

This was a large 'area' gathering which attracted a crowd and we walked there annually with our parents, and the pram.

*****

ELLESMERE WORKHOUSE

Generally, old people who became too ill to care for themselves properly, were admitted to Ellesmere Workhouse, and spent their remaining days there. Myddle people seldom entered this shelter, however, as there was frequently a nearby caring relative to look after them in those days.

Very occasionally, if a young village girl became pregnant, and the man concerned refused to marry her (or could not) she had no option but to seek refuge at the Workhouse. The baby invariably entered an orphanage, and the girl returned to farm or domestic service.

Girls were commonly banished from home in disgrace in these circumstances, without a penny in their pocket, and were obliged to walk to Ellesmere, a few precious belongings wrapped in a newspaper under their arm. There they stayed, until the baby was born. The Workhouse Administrator, meanwhile, endeavoured to make the unfortunate girl surrender the name of the father, so that an order for maintenance might be applied for. If successful, the court order was in the region of 7/6d per week, depending on the young man's earnings, and this payment continued until the child was 14 years old.

When it was known that a maintenance order existed, the girl's family, who had previously condemned her to the Workhouse, could have an abrupt change of mind, and suddenly be eager to take back daughter, baby, and the new weekly income!

CHAPTER NINE

Ordering the Estate

'The rich man in his castle,
The poor man at his gate –
He made them, high or lowly,
And ordered their estate.'
Mrs C F Alexander 1823-95
– a verse (no longer used) from the hymn
'All things bright and beautiful.'

Sales or transfers of property by the landed classes could have far-reaching effects on whole families in a village, in the days when most property was attached to estates owned by the various gentry. Certainly much upheaval was caused when the estate which included our cottage was sold in 1920 or thereabouts.

The landlords notified tenants, including Father, that the estate was to be sold, and tenants would be given the opportunity to purchase their cottages. The general rule was that the cottages would be offered to tenants first; if they could not afford to buy, farmers purchased them for their employees. Many farmworkers consequently did not move. But this was entirely at the discretion of the owners and their agents; real hardship could be caused where tenants (perhaps with many years' residence and nowhere else to turn) might have their own homes sold to other parties.

I will explain what happened to the cottages of our family and some of our neighbours, as it shows how even in the 1920s, landowners had the 'whip hand' over the low-waged villagers, and were thus able to impose their values on the whole working population. Aunt Ethel, with her recent inheritance, let it be known that she was interested in our dwelling. She knew Father had little hope of buying it, with his large family and a low farm-labourer's wage of 12/6d per week. She was quite right, of course; my parents had no savings whatsoever. Our cottage was in an attractive position with much land.

However, one Tom Roberts, a bachelor of Myddle Timber Yard, suggested that he and Father go to the sale together. They had served at the same camp during the war years and subsequently become good friends. Prior to the appointed time for the sale, which was to be held in the club room over the stables at the *Red Lion*, Tom and Father sat in our parlour and watched Ethel go by, on her way to the sale.

An event of unparalleled importance (as this was) called, they felt, for their best Sunday suits, white shirts, celluloid collars and black ties. They followed Ethel. She was surprised to see them.

Our cottage rent had hitherto been twenty-four-shillings per quarter, paid personally by Mother on quarter days at the club room.

The land agents, representing Lord Brownlow of Ellesmere, sat behind a trestle table facing the gathered tenants. It was these agents who were to assess the values of properties and how much each tenant should be requested to pay.

Eventually, they came to our cottage:

ROSE COTTAGE, occupied by Henry Ebrey.
A 4-roomed dwelling in central village position.
Field and large vegetable garden. Wash house.

Mr Ebrey worked for the estate, as had his father before him. He had served his country during the war, etc. A price of £90 was agreed by the agents.

Whether the tenants were employees of the estate, and if they had 'served their country' in the recent Great War, were important factors in deciding if the prices of cottages or holdings would be fixed at levels reasonable and affordable by the tenants. Father scored well on both these points; so the sale price of our cottage was fairly low.

Tom Roberts offered to lend Father the £90, and this was settled verbally between them in a matter of seconds. No solicitors were involved; it was simply agreed on the spot, on the basis that Father would repay the loan when he could.

This was how we came to purchase 'Rose Cottage'. My parents had little idea how they would repay a £90 loan on earnings of 12/6d per week, which was not enough to even feed us properly, never mind paying for a house; although we were lucky that things did improve in a few years.

Helen outside Rose Cottage. Behind the wall was an old school bench with an enamel bowl for washing. Cottages lacked bathrooms and toilets, so children often washed out of doors in all weather, without too much regard for privacy.

The next property to be considered was the one next door to us, occupied by uncle Jack (Grice). Records showed that Jack was the village lengthman and had worked all his life on the estate. Jack obviously expected to get his cottage for £90. However, the agents drew a distinction here, and implied that as Mr Grice had *not* served under arms, he should pay £140, which he refused outright, storming out of the gathering in a temper which was quite out of character. This cottage was similar to ours but included a joined-on building used for storage.

The agents did not reconsider their offer, however; the owner of one of the village farms was allowed to purchase the cottage, and it was converted into two cottages for his employees. Jack and his family had to move!

Aunt Ethel's cottage was offered to her for £100, mention being made of the fact that she had served her country during the war. Although a good way from the village, and if anything closer to Harmer Hill, the dwelling was large, with much land annexed, and aunt seemed pleased with the transaction. So she remained where she was.

As the sale continued, little interest was shown in the cottage rented by Mr Husbands (senior), Ethel's father-in-law, which occupied an unrivalled position on Myddle Hill (and still does), near the top of the 'Gullet'. The asking price for this property was only £70, because it and its garden were relatively small. Ethel enquired if she might buy this too, so that old Mr Husbands could spend the remainder of his days in familiar and agreeable surroundings, and this the agents consented to.

Regrettably, old Mr Husbands died soon after the sale, while uncle Jack was still in his cottage next door, under notice, searching for other accommodation. So Ethel invited Jack (her brother-in-law) to become her tenant, for a very modest weekly rent – this arrangement worked amicably. There were originally two adjoining cottages at this site, but the one on the west side was demolished to make way for two new houses which were built on the land released plus the garden, on Myddle Hill.

Granny's cottage in the Gullet was rented from the estate, as was that of her neighbour, Granny Walford. They had lived next door to each other for their entire married lives, both raising large families in unbelievably cramped conditions. Granny Walford's eldest son now lived in Crewe; upon learning that the estate was to be sold, he was quite naturally concerned for his mother's welfare, so he journeyed to Myddle to attend the sale.

When the two properties concerned came up for discussion, Mr Walford spoke, representing both old ladies. He stated that my late grandfather and the late Mr Walford had both worked on the estate, and he wished to purchase the two cottages, so that Granny Walford and Granny Ebrey could remain for the rest of their lives in the homes they loved, in the Gullet. The agents agreed to this arrangement, and it was through the generosity of Mr Walford that my granny lived rent-free for the remainder of her life.

Granny Ebrey in the doorway of her small cottage in the Gullet, long-demolished, in which she raised six children. She would have been evicted when the estate was sold in her old age, but for the generosity of a neighbour's son.

After purchase of our cottage, there began a long struggle to repay the money to Tom Roberts. To this end Father did many extra seasonal jobs when they were available. Meanwhile Tom moved to London; Father posted sums of money, as and when he could, which always included the cash from the sale of our damsons and earnings from any extra harvesting work. It was to be many years before the debt was finally repaid.

*****

Of course it was quite usual in those days, especially in farming communities, for children of poor families to work part-time, to help pay the bills.

Having to pay off this huge loan on the cottage simply made our finances even more difficult than they would have been anyway.

One of my many tasks was to deliver three cans of fresh milk daily, which I collected from Castle Farm early in the morning, before school. (I was always called at 6am, before the other children, to help Mother light the range for hot water to make tea, and help prepare Father's breakfast and sandwiches for lunch.) I delivered this milk to the schoolmaster, the shopkeeper and young Mr Painter and they each paid me 2d per week for this service. This was long before we had bottled milk in the countryside; the milk was carried in special 1-pint enamel cans, which must seem unhygienic by the standards of today.

I also delivered telegrams for Mrs Bourne, the postmistress, for which I received 1½d for local deliveries within the village. The 'system' was that Mrs Bourne told Mother that a telegram was awaiting delivery; Mother then came to the school playground during break and passed the message to me. If the telegram was for Shotton Hall [which later became Shotton Hall School for maladjusted boys], I would ask Mr Porch if I might leave school a little early because of the distance. He usually agreed, especially in winter-time, and I went straight to the post office before commencing the tedious walk to the south-east side of Harmer Hill, for which I was paid 9d. (Telegrams were never really treated with any particular urgency, as is apparent from these slow procedures. No doubt the senders had paid good money for immediate delivery.) Upon presenting the envelope at the tradesman's entrance, a kindly butler would arrange for me to have a slice of apple pie or fruit-cake, whichever was available, but this I was instructed to hide under my coat until clear of the grounds.

On one such visit I actually met the Marchioness herself. The butler directed me to the hot-houses where she was inspecting work. I curtsied when I found her – she was quite alone – and offered the telegram. She read it, and said there would be no reply. (I also delivered telegrams to farms.)

I carried water from the well twice weekly to three folk who lived in the Gullet. This was not the easy task that it may sound, for the bucket was very heavy and there was nowhere that I could rest it for a moment because of the Gullet's sloping sides. My remuneration for this particularly laborious task totalled 6d per week.

To help the family finances yet further, we became newspaper deliverers. The papers, *Wellington Journal* on a Saturday and *Oswestry Observer* on a Wednesday, were brought to our home on the first bus. The delivery girls were usually Emily, Elsie and myself, and we carried a little book of addresses of where they had to be taken. The newspapers then cost 1½d each, and this money we had to collect, but usually farmers left the money in the front porch, so we never saw anyone. Mostly we split up and went in different directions, but when we delivered to the few scattered cottages and two farms known as Wackley, we all stayed together. Mother insisted upon this because we were so far from home, and she feared that the money we had collected might be stolen. On the return walk, when we reached the quaint bell-towered chapel at Burlton village, we took the little lane which ran behind. Here, from a wooden hut in her garden, old Mrs Gwilt sold margarine at 4d per lb, and when the weather was moderately cool we bought 2lbs for Mother, as this commodity was not available in our village. We were allowed to spend 2d on sweets as a special concession by Mother for walking such a distance.

The other local newspaper was the *Shrewsbury Chronicle*, but the inhabitants of Myddle and its hinterland favoured the *Wellington Journal,* which was cheaper and carried both national and world news. This paper also covered local fêtes and marriages, and carried many advertisements for cures to a variety of ailments with which agricultural workers might be afflicted.

Earlier I mentioned Myddlewood Reading Room, where poor Mary Grice had taken me to dances before she was stricken by tuberculosis. The Reading Room was in regular use when I was young, and in fact served as a village hall, being maintained by the parish. Old men went along to read the weekly newspaper and have a smoke and chat. The wooden building was cleaned regularly and a large iron stove was lit to keep it warm. It contained a compact kitchen; a supply of tables and chairs were at hand which could be used for weddings, dances, whist drives and an occasional concert of local talent organised by the church. It was eventually closed and demolished.

*****

In September we all helped pick the fruits of the countryside in the old quarry and along the pretty winding lanes, now with the slightest tint of autumn in evidence. When full, our baskets were carried to a small market-garden at Myddlewood run by the Misses Ratcliffe. We were paid 1/6d for each basket and these were then taken into market. One sister was more competent when driving their horse and trap and it fell to her to take the load. There were three sisters and I delivered the *Oswestry Observer* to them every Wednesday and was always rewarded with a piece of cake. (One remembers these things!)

Even the one shilling piece passed through the railway carriage window to me by father's sister, aunt Lizzie, had to be handed over to Mother. It was my reward for helping her carry baskets of damsons to Yorton Station after her annual visit to grandmother, from Crewe.

All the money which we earned, or were given, had to be passed on to Mother who placed it in an old metal tea caddy, placed high on a shelf over the range. A small source of ready cash was thus always available to pay calling tradesmen: for the purchase of oil for the lamps, brawn on Fridays, bread, etc.

Knitting was another means of earning extra cash, and was an occupation which called upon Mother's creative skills. She was something of an expert, having been taught when quite young by her adoptive mother. She never used a pattern but was capable of making clothes in lovely single-coloured designs. Only dark wools in three colours (brown, black and navy) were available in those days. She carried intricate patterns in her head, and word of her skills spread to Harmer Hill where she acquired a regular customer, a chemist's wife. Mother supplied this lady with smart ivory silk frocks for evening wear, worked in a basket-stitch design for the bodice, with huge bat-wing sleeves (which have again become fashionable today). The dress had a lacy patterned skirt with pretty scalloped hem. Afternoon frocks followed the same basic style but were knitted in dark wools. A frock would take about one week to knit, which Mother did mainly in the evenings by the light of the oil lamp. She made a charge of 10 shillings for an art silk frock, which included the cost of the silk. A favourite outfit of this customer was a skirt knitted to form pleats with a matching jumper with no welt, which rolled up at the waist. To complement each outfit Mother knitted stockings which were knee length, in the same silk/wool.

We were rewarded with a rarely-seen orange when we delivered completed outfits to this kindly lady.

If work was a bit slack, we were sent round the village with samples of Mother's knitting wrapped carefully in a *Wellington Journal*. We were usually successful in obtaining a few orders, mainly for children's jumpers.

When socks wore out at the heels because of the amount of walking everyone did, she cut off the sock above the heel, picked up the stitches and re-knit the foot. This was done a few times to the same pair, as the welt remained in good condition up to the knee. Many orders were received for this re-heeling work, which was far less expensive than buying a new pair.

Mother diligently knitted socks for farmers' children (she was paid 8d per pair which enabled her to buy more wool). She also made warm shawls in thick wool for old ladies with rheumaticky shoulders; these had a pretty scalloped edge and were always requested in black. The wool was sold in hanks and some were monsters to unwind. Her source of wool was a tiny shop in Wem run by a Miss Hope, where it could be purchased at 1½d or 2d per ounce.

One of Mother's customers persuaded her to enter a competition advertised in the *Wellington Journal* and organised by a Yorkshire wool mill, for a hand-knit jumper. Mother won 8oz of wool for entering the competition, and her knitting gained a 'highly commended' certificate when returned! We helped by making the pom-poms and tassels which decorated many items, by filling small cardboard circles with wool until the hole in the centre disappeared.

Another task which Mother undertook was that of school cleaner, which involved general cleaning and lighting of fires. During the school holidays we all helped her and worked extra hard, scrubbing the floors and the area around the pump outside.

Emily and I were regularly sent to fetch logs from the coppices and woods to stoke the school stoves. We were despatched on this task late at night, so that no-one would see us. Father then chopped the wood up in the parlour in front of the fire, and that is how the lovely green tiles of the Victorian fireplace became cracked and broken. Mother took the wood to school early next morning to light the old stoves.

Casual work for women was provided by farmers, which involved milking cows early in the morning, before children went to school, and again in the early evening after school. Older children looked after younger brothers and sisters while mother was away, and a small wage was paid for this work.

Father did many odd jobs and was glad of any work offered to him. One of these was emptying the Schoolmaster's earth closet, every three months or so, for which he received 1/6d, apparently the standard remuneration for emptying closets – it was of course a deeply unpleasant job.

In this way, starting while Father was still only earning 12/6d per week as a farm labourer, the whole family helped to bring in enough income both to keep us all alive and start paying off the seemingly-impossible sum of £90 for our cottage.

Work availability improved further for Father. He obtained employment with Salop County Council, working on the construction of Shrewsbury By-Pass and small contracts involving the re-surfacing of roads, etc. During this period, he worked on the construction of the new concrete bridge at Atcham, cycling the 11 miles or so each way. This bridge was eventually opened on 24 October 1929 by the then-Minister of Transport, Herbert Morrison MP. The bridge has attractive concrete balustrades and five large arch spans. Graceful though this bridge is, and glad as I was that Father had helped in its construction, albeit only as a labourer, to my mind the old bridge is far more beautiful.

The earlier bridge, built 1769-71, which stands alongside the new one, was constructed of white stone, with decorative key stones and has seven arches with cutwaters at the base, persuading the water to flow around, rather than undermine the stone. The designer was John Gwynn of Shrewsbury, a friend of Dr Johnson and a founder member of the Royal Academy. He also built Magdalen Bridge at Oxford. The overall appearance of the site is quite dramatic, with the two graceful bridges standing side by side; steam lorries and petrol cars now diverting to the new bridge on their long journey from London to Holyhead (via a considerable section of the old Roman Road – Watling Street).

Whilst Father worked on the construction of the new bridge he earned 30 shillings per week, which was a good wage.

CHAPTER TEN

The Mole-Catcher's Daughter

One of my dearest and closest friends throughout childhood (and again later in life when we corresponded with each other) was Marjorie Painter.

She lived a little further down the quarry lane in one of the oldest and most beautiful thatched cottages in the whole of Myddle. A single-storey gem! It was entered via an old oak gate with exotic peacocks clipped from yew, standing on each side. These were the only examples of topiary in the village, and were accordingly objects of delight and curiosity. Mr Painter was rather proud of these.

Another delightful feature was the path that led to their front door. Unlike other cobbles laid in the vicinity, the paver had taken time and methodically laid the smooth small stones in decorative designs.

I have referred above to the low thatch, which hung almost to head-height. This proved a constant worry to Marjorie's mother who was concerned that a spark from their chimney might set the roof alight. Ever mindful of this, buckets were always on hand which could be quickly filled from the running brook at their garden boundary.

William Painter, the village mole-catcher, outside his cottage in the 1930s. The cottage still stands – no longer thatched, and unrecognisable beneath a modern surface.

William Painter, Marjorie's father, was a mole and rabbit catcher by trade and farmers called on horseback or by horse and trap when his services were required. He was kept busy, as moles caused devastation to farm land.

I often watched with interest as he pinned the mole-skins tightly to a board in the curing process. When fully cured he despatched them by post to a furrier in Knightsbridge (London), where Myddle mole and rabbit skins were transformed into elegant coats for fashionable London women. His sons also followed their father's trade and became mole-catchers.

Marjorie's mother, Emma, was one of those rare ladies ready and eager to nurse people, or lend a hand generally if anyone was ill. She helped the doctor or nurse during childbirths and assisted mothers with young babies. She was always sent for after a farm accident, and someone else would go to Grinshill to fetch the doctor. Mrs Painter knew exactly what to do until the doctor arrived.

When she made wines and beer we helped Marjorie fill a churn with water at the pump, and then push it on a strange 3-wheel truck round to her cottage.

Mr Painter kept pigs and ferrets, and Marjorie fetched their straw from Castle Farm on a barrow. This was hard work for a girl, and old 'Nat' used to pile it up high and laugh at her efforts to push the load. Mrs Painter, meanwhile, reared calves until they were young heifers. Their field extended from behind the cottage along the quarry lane, almost to the old quarry. [New houses have long since covered all remains of it]. She then drove the heifers to Wem market, with a few friends who did the same. They began to walk with the animals at 7am. Mr Painter and his sons went along too, as the cattle wandered anywhere once out on the lanes and were difficult to control. While the animals were being fattened ready for Wem, the children had to cut up turnips when they came home from school, to last the cattle all day. There was always so much to do, it used to be a race as to what they did first!

Another example of the closely-knit community spirit which existed in those days was shown by Mrs Boliver, her neighbour across the lane. She was only too glad to let Mrs Painter use the bread oven in her wash-house, whenever she needed to. And here Mrs Painter baked volumes of bread for her family.

Marjorie's brother, Stanley, married a Buildwas girl and they settled at Bagley. When they all went over to see Stanley's baby, they hired a horse and trap from Mr Mullinux. Marjorie was a little fearful of these excursions however. She was apprehensive that the horse might bolt, or fall, and the hump-back canal bridge at Shade Oak, which the horse took at a trot, was quite a terrifying experience for her.

She returned after these visits with stories of the old canal. Most village children had no knowledge of a canal, even though an old branch of the Shropshire Union had terminated at Westonwharf, a mere 4 miles away from Myddle. Nobody had a map or atlas at home in those days to study. In fact very few homes contained books at all, except a bible. So it fell to Marjorie to relate her concept of a canal, as we gathered around her in the school playground, eager to learn first-hand.

She had observed horse-drawn barges near Bagley, bringing cargoes for the whole area.

It appeared to us from her description that a canal, to all intents and purposes, much resembled a river, but was narrower with a path (called a tow-path) for the horse to pull the barge. Walkers were required to stand aside to allow the huge horse to pass.

Also, she related that 'bargees' were in charge and lived on board with their families.

Bagley people were able to take pleasant evening strolls for as far as they wished. This was an agreeable place to stroll away from the dusty lanes used by carts.

Later Marjorie spent all her holidays at Bagley, brother Stanley fetching her on his bike and Marjorie sitting on a cushion tied to the crossbar.

Marjorie and I left school at about the same time, but like me, she could only get the usual low wages for local occupations. She first went to Burlton Grange Farm for a month; moving to Stanwardine Farm and then to Grange Farm at Bomere Heath. Her next move was away from Shropshire altogether, to the city of Manchester and a pork butcher's shop where she earned the princely sum of 25 shillings per week (about five times what she could earn in Shropshire). Her landlady, however, took 18 shillings of this for her lodgings. Mr Allen, her kindly employer, thought this excessive and set to work to convert the attic over the shop into a little bedroom. When complete it was very cosy. After 14 months Marjorie became homesick for the countryside and her family and returned to work at Grange Farm, Bomere Heath.

Sadly, at 19, Marjorie contracted a serious illness and it was necessary to give up heavy work for a time. So she set up as Agent for a mail-order catalogue company based in Manchester.

She took orders for goods from the catalogues all around the village, and worked on a commission basis. She did very well, as the low-paid farmworkers' families found it advantageous to pay for necessities weekly or monthly, and this method also dispensed with the difficult journeys to the shops at Shrewsbury. The only disadvantage was that women purchasing clothing from the catalogue company began to lose their individuality to a degree, as the choice of clothes was limited and many began to dress in the same styles, albeit the colours differed somewhat. This was one of the influences which tended to standardise styles of clothing, helping to make grandmother's old shawls etc look so outdated.

Furniture also became available from the catalogue company. A special 'Bedding Set' proved immensely popular, especially to young women engaged to be married. It consisted of two blankets, two sheets, two pillow cases and a cotton quilt, all for the bargain price of £1. Until this time village women had sewn their own eiderdowns and some still did.

There had been an initiative earlier in this direction when the Reverend Woolward's wife saw a need for such a scheme. She operated two clubs: a Coal Club and a Clothing Club. Villagers paid what they could afford for 12 months and Mrs Woolward gave them each a bonus; the shops in Shrewsbury involved in the scheme also allowed a bonus. Yates of Baschurch were the merchants involved in the coal club, and the same system of a double bonus applied.

Marjorie eventually married, raised a family and lived in Myddle. We continued to write until her demise.

CHAPTER ELEVEN

The Queen and the Gentry

During the two unhappy years that Emily and I worked in fear of our lives, an event took place at St Peter's church that was to make village history.

The Queen of England HRH Queen Mary (formerly Mary of Teck now wife of the monarch, King George V) attended morning worship. The year would be about 1926. She was visiting her brother, the Marquess of Cambridge (Prince of Teck, until German names went out of fashion in 1914). The Queen was accompanied by her sister-in-law, the Marchioness. There was great excitement in the village and I was permitted to leave my farm duties for a mere half-hour to join the crowd gathered outside the church.

I stood quite close to the Queen as she left by the north door, sweeping past us, looking very beautiful in a long grey brocade dress and carrying a matching parasol. A pill-box type hat rested lightly on her greying hair. The hat was trimmed with clusters of grey and lavender velvet flowers, and a small grey veil covered her forehead. She smiled pleasantly to the large crowd which had formed and waved as she left by car. The Reverend Nesbitt (who had succeeded the Reverend Woolward) and his French-born wife, were invited to join the Queen for lunch at Shotton Hall.

Our friend Annie, who was now a choir-girl on Sundays, had the privilege of being seated inside the church, in a position forward of the pews. The church was filled to capacity.

Queen Mary made certain courtesy calls during her stay at Shotton Hall. These were to prominent titled families nearby and included the Lady Mary Doyne at Marton Hall. (Village rumour had it that the staff were provided with new uniforms for the occasion, and lined the great hall as the Queen entered.) The Queen also visited Lord Bibby at Sansaw Hall near Grinshill.

Activity at Yorton Station prior to the Queen's visit was intense. As a small contingency, a hastily constructed waiting room, in dark greyish brick, was built on the west platform. It was considered by railway officials that if the weather should be inclement, the Queen would require somewhere to take shelter while the Royal Train pulled out of the station, as she would have to cross the track to gain access to the yard and waiting cars. Popular belief is, however, that the Queen didn't actually enter this snug little room at all: instead she chatted to the reception party on the platform, while the train pulled away. But that was how Yorton Station got a waiting-room on the Crewe-bound platform!

But to return to my childhood, in 1918, or thereabouts, the new residents at Marton Hall were the Lord and Lady Gosling. Her Ladyship eagerly became a generous benefactor in the village and organised events which brought undiluted pleasure to poor country children.

One of her initial treats was a Christmas party at the Hall for children of school age. Her numerous uniformed servants made us welcome and provided a dainty tea served on starched white tablecloths. We were seated in resplendent surroundings.

Afterwards we moved to another larger room, in the centre of which stood a giant pine-scented Christmas tree, extending to the ceiling of the lofty room. Its outstretched branches were decorated with hundreds of candles and a brightly wrapped gift for each child. Her Ladyship told us that her three sons had been responsible for wrapping all the gifts and labelling them. She invited us to walk around the tree until we discovered our name on a parcel, then one of her sons would untie it. The gifts were extravagant, mine being a set of wooden doll's furniture expertly carved by a craftsman.

And her generosity did not end here. When the party games were over and we were about to commence the long walk home, she produced crackers, parcels of sweets, chocolates and an orange, in fact we had too much to carry and some of these precious items found themselves undeservedly stuffed into old coat pockets.

Lady Gosling's next inspiration was a spectacular summer outing to Rhyl. She knew that village children had been denied any opportunity to see the sea. In those days neither the school, nor the church (nor anyone else) thought to arrange any kind of outing beyond the Shropshire boundary, so poorer children had no chance ever to travel to other parts of the country.

For this excursion three magnificent 'White Rose' charabancs were hired from a garage at Oswestry. Her Ladyship arrived at school promptly in horse and trap to witness our grand departure (as indeed did anyone not engaged upon their labour that morning – for charabancs were rarely seen in the heart of the village). She gave us all sweets for the long journey.

My most vivid memory of this seaside resort, were the pretty cane basket chairs, with throne-like high curved backs, unexpectedly placed in clusters along the sands.

Thanks to this generous Lady in Myddle, we experienced for the first time, drinking tea in a cafe, eating a meal in a restaurant, a boat trip (with Miss Cank being carried, protesting and blushing, by the boatman down a plank to the waiting boat, many inches of lace petticoat exposed). We saw and heard giant sea-gulls, gathered shells, sifted the fine sand through our fingers, and smelt the salty air. It was all so unbelievably different, like being in another world. I found the great mass of grey sea-water quite frightening, and much preferred the gentle meres and pools at home, which we explored annually on Good Friday. It was certainly an undeniably exciting day – one which we would remember all our lives.

Lord Gosling had a friendly greeting for everyone as he walked briskly to morning worship at St Peter's every Sunday.

When his three sons were home from Eton, they accompanied him. Dressed in their Eton uniforms and each carrying an umbrella, they amused the village lads no end! The whole village was distressed when it was announced that the family were moving to Scotland.

Marton Hall's next distinguished occupant was Lady Mary Doyne, who was equally generous in her ways, and is still remembered for her many good deeds in our small community. My youngest sister, Dorothy, attended many parties at the Hall. An especially memorable one, devised by her Ladyship, occurred one Eastertime. She had arranged for numerous silver-wrapped chocolate eggs to be concealed in the trees and shrubs of the garden. Children were invited to search for the appropriate egg labelled with their name. Dorothy's moment of delight was marred slightly as her egg was in a high branch and she had to wait for a tall girl to retrieve it. Chocolate eggs had evaded the village shop, as Lady Doyne knew only too well.

Regrettably, this lovely person died from a heart attack while only in her forties.

A large crowd attended the funeral. Mother's foot was tightly bandaged, following the removal of a toe, so she and Dorothy kept a little distance from the mourners. Lady Doyne's coffin was conveyed to church on a haycart, drawn with dignity by a team of well-groomed wagon horses. Wreaths were piled on the coffin top and spilled over onto the cart.

Members of my family paid their respects in the churchyard later, when it was quiet and the mourners had dispersed. My sister wept, as this remarkable Lady had exuded kindness to everyone, but especially to deprived local children. The fragrant scent from blooms of hundreds of sweet peas, forming a border around the grave, hung on the air. The gardeners from the hall had painstakingly prepared a special display and now, with the wreaths laid in the centre, not an inch of freshly dug earth was visible.

CHAPTER TWELVE

Granny Ebrey of the Gullet

Granny Ebrey, my father's mother, lived at the first of the sandstone cottages on the north side of the Gullet, which path I was fond of walking through as a child, straddling it with one leg on each side. The Gullet was a local antiquity; a path of natural rock, uneven and steep into which a narrow water-channel had worn away the stone when finding its own passage down the gradient. This unique cottage access route was an interesting topographical feature. (In the terraced-cottage next door lived Granny's life-long friend, Granny Walford.)

My granny's dwelling was tiny, but always neat, and very much older than our cottage. It possessed only one modest living room, which accommodated the iron range with its assortment of smoke-blackened cooking pots suspended from hooks and chains over the fire.

A large wash-house adjoined the outside west wall of the cottage, with a built-in brick boiler. Granny filled this for washing, with water collected in a wooden butt and drained from the roof. A fire was lit underneath, and a little door closed. The brick foundation retained heat for some time after use, and during the winter, washing was hung round to dry. This wash-house also served as a bathroom for granny's large family, helping to alleviate congestion in the small living room.

Thus had washing been done in the village of Myddle back in the previous century.

A narrow oak staircase led up from the main room

directly into a bedroom. The bed in the centre was almost as large as the room it occupied. From this chamber was a door to a second, slightly larger room where there was space for a little furniture in addition to two beds. Two large polished tin trunks stood one on top of the other, containing best clothes. Winter clothes were usually folded neatly and packed into the lower trunk with mothballs. Over the top granny draped a pretty hand-embroidered white linen cloth.

Everyday clothes were hung behind the door. A table housed a jug, bowl and soap dish, which were only used by the district nurse during times of illness.

[Both these cottages have long been demolished; a dwelling of the 1980s, in 1980s style, towers over the site. The Gullet itself has been surfaced and partly replaced by a modern flight of steps.]

Children were expected to leave home at the age of 14, when they left school, and live at the farm or large house where they had obtained employment; thus space in a bed became available for a younger child at this tiny dwelling. Later, upon marriage, young couples became eligible for a farm cottage, and often sisters made their home with newly-married couples if conditions were impossibly cramped at home. This was how the problem of severe overcrowding was overcome to some extent.

Granny bore six children – four girls and two boys (just as there were four surviving girls and two boys in my family). I never knew my grandfather, who had died suddenly from a heart attack whilst digging in his garden at the age of 44. He had worked as head-gardener at Petton Hall, a mansion some two miles north-west of Myddle.

To make ends meet, granny cleaned for Mr Jones, who then ran the store. She was a devout Christian, honest and hard-working. She worked so well for Mr Jones that this kindly man made provision for her by way of a bequest of 12/6d per week, covered legally in his will, so that after his death she would continue to have a regular income for the remainder of her life.

This helped to keep herself and her grandson (Bill), who lived with her, after her own children had all left home.

Granny was always neat in appearance, in her long black frock, white apron, black woollen shawl and dainty white cotton bonnet, the strings of which were often untied as she busied herself in her little home. The sight of women dressed uniformly in this rustic Victorian style, and the contrast of black and white, was quite dramatic.

The low sandstone wall, which ran from her gate to her door, indicated her boundary with granny Walford's cottage, and we regularly scrubbed the top of this wall for her. Some of the stones had hollows, where little bottoms had sat over the years! We kept the top of the wall clean as she draped washing here to dry in the sun. An old iron horse-shoe hung near her door, which one of her sons found whilst working in the fields.

She regularly purchased supplies of Whixall peat at 1/6d a sack from a middle-aged lady who drove a horse and cart to the village. Whixall peat burned well, and was used by many inhabitants as fuel. The woman had to carry the sacks from Myddle Bank, on her back, to granny's wash-house for storage,

In the 1980s, the last remaining cottage in the Gullet shows the same simple architectural style as Granny Ebrey's – albeit disguised by a modern textured surface – and having the same round-edged sandstone front-garden walls. The modern-day Gullet is a smooth tarmac path, very different from the rough-hewn irregular path of Granny's day.

because of the difficult terrain of the Gullet. This path was not accessible to a horse and cart in either direction.

Peat was still burned instead of coal in those days, since it was usually cheaper than delivered coal in areas fairly close to a peat moss. Logs were usually even cheaper, when they could be obtained.

Granny attended many of the garden fêtes and village events and was one of the oldest inhabitants (being in her 90s). She brought all her children up in the Christian faith, quoting them passages from her bible which she knew by heart.

Special church services were held on Wednesday evenings, after which alms, in the form of bread (not always fresh), were distributed from the vestry door to the poor people of the parish. This bread was first blessed by the rector. Several boards depicting names of benefactors who had provided charitable donations (with the sums provided) were displayed on the vestry wall. Granny, being so old, qualified for such alms, which she gave to me for Mother. We were always glad of it.

When very old, granny became almost blind (as did other female members of my family, as a result of a lifetime of sewing and darning by the light of oil lamps), so we children accompanied her to worship. This was an especially delightful task on a winter evening, as we carried her 'special lamp', with candle inside, each child supporting her as we led her through the village. For church she wore a long black woollen cloak, which had thousands of jet beads worked in intricate floral patterns decorating it. A little bonnet of the same material complemented her outfit.

Often when we called for her, we would find her fast asleep in the old rocking-chair by the fire. She didn't always have time to get changed, but the moment we helped her on with the cloak and bonnet, an unbelievable transformation took place. The jets caught the light from the flickering candles and oil lamps inside the church, and we felt so proud of our distinctively-dressed granny, and privileged to be in her company.

Grandfather lay in the churchyard under the little fir tree

now blown towards the east by a century of prevailing west winds across the plain. This tree still stands to the right of the lych gate and, 50 years later, granny joined him at the same spot. Little baby Beatrice lies at their feet – I will tell you about her later.

No stone marks their resting-place. We just know our grandparents and baby sister are there.

Footnote: According to village gossip it was said that granny was born out of wedlock. She was said to be the child of the master and cook of the 'great house' – but no one seemed to know which one. I can only comment that she worked hard, raised six children; her husband having died young. She was a wonderful hard working, good-living, gran.

Her daughter Elizabeth (Lizzie) bore a son, out of wedlock, during the war. Granny cared for the boy, Bill, who had a good voice and sang in the church choir.

Lizzie married a railway worker and moved to Crewe, and she kept in touch with her family.

CHAPTER THIRTEEN

Our Postman/Cobbler/Sexton/Clerk

His tombstone really tells us very little about him:

In Loving Memory of
William Wright
Clerk and Sexton of this Parish
for 36 years

Who died 24 June 1938 aged 73 years

Life's Work Well Done

We also knew him as the Postman. He was a seasoned walker who refused to succumb to suggestions that a bike might ease his work-load – but he actually used a stout wooden wheelbarrow on Christmas Day because of the load of parcels which had to be delivered. In those days the Christmas post was actually delivered on Christmas Day. Mr Wright was not a drinking man, but he always got through a fair quantity of home-made wine during his Christmas Day round.

He walked many miles, in all weathers. Often he would be the only link with Myddle and inhabitants of isolated cottages before the era of public transport, radio or telephone.

This versatile gentleman was also the village cobbler and found time, between postal rounds, to repair boots in a neat little hut behind his cottage. He never married, and lived with his brother Fred, a farmworker, and their sister Emma, who was their housekeeper. They lived up on Myddle Hill which, although only some 330ft above sea level, its position was such as to allow tremendous views across the plain lying to the north-east. Their cottage, 'Ingle Nook' was quite delightful and deserves mention for, although tiny, with low thatch and exposed beams, its position on the roadside considerably enhanced this stretch of the top highway. It was a favourite with children because of its perfect dimensions.

Mother had taken us inside for a look around at a time when the cottage had been vacant. I recall a staircase led to a square landing, which might just about accommodate a small bed and be used as a spare bedroom. The main bedroom led off and was dark with only a small window at each end, one facing north and the other peeping down over rear gardens and the winding village street. There were exposed beams at intervals which supported the roof. From memory the chimney was on the outside and could well have been added at a period after construction for the cottage was very old. [In 1951, Ellesmere Rural District Council had recommended a Grade III Listing for this restored black and white cottage as a building of architectural or historic interest. Sadly, however, after habitation by generation after generation, it was condemned and demolished in 1966.

Likewise at the same time, 1951, Castle Farm, was also recommended for Grade III listing. Villagers were dismayed when this historic building in the centre of the village, which was L-shaped and incorporated a timber frame, was demolished in 1963, and permission granted for a new modern dwelling to replace it.]

I called often at 'Ingle Nook' to collect Father's boots and boots for other people who paid me 2d for this errand. I was invited inside by Miss Emma Wright, to wait. The room was enchanting, with interesting objects everywhere upon which I feasted my eyes, hoping that the boots might not be quite ready. Miss Wright's open bag of embroidery lay on the red velvet-fringed tablecloth; she was obviously preparing for the next sale of work. Three comfortable old arm-chairs were positioned round the fireplace/oven, complete with white linen antimacassars embroidered by Emma. The heavy black cast-iron grate incorporated an iron grid, fabricated at the forge, which hooked on the front for cooking and keeping food warm. All shined and gleamed with a brightness indicative of regular, loving cleaning with grate polish. The oven doors, which opened with large brass knobs, had an embossed pattern shaped like clusters of grapes.

The setting was complemented with gleaming brass fender and companion set (tongs, shovel, poker and brush, all with brass handles); also Emma's finely embroidered mantle-shelf cover, which hid from view the socks and other airing clothes hanging beneath. This fireplace with its embellishments made the whole room look beautiful.

But not only was Mr Wright our postman and cobbler, he was also clerk and sexton of the parish for many years. There were obviously times when he was too busy to perform all the duties required of a sexton, so Father, a regular churchgoer was asked to help out.

One of the many duties involved lighting the fire for the church's heating system. This consisted of a fire-place in a small sandstone hut built into the churchyard wall near Castle Farm. Pipes from the back of this fire-place ran across the churchyard, entering the church on the east side. We all loved helping Father with this job, lighting the fire on a Friday night after he had prepared it.

We could then be seen in all weathers, purposeful expressions upon our faces, as we hurried through the village, coats pulled over our heads, to stoke the fire at intervals all through Saturday so that the church would be tolerably warm by Sunday. How much heat was lost between fireplace and church, and how much it cost to heat the church for Sunday services by means of a coal fire started up the previous Friday, we never knew.

Father was trained by Mr Wright to ring the bells (there were three), dig graves, act as witness at weddings, attend funerals, and assist generally in the running of St Peter's. His first grave-digging assignment was very nearly his last! Measurements of the excavation required had been passed to him, but due to some unaccountable error, he had omitted to allow the necessary 2-3 inches required to clear the coffin. The funeral in question was that of a well-known member of the community, hence a larger number of mourners than usual were in attendance. Trouble came at the graveside when the coffin was lowered – it simply would not fit, despite desperate efforts on the part of the undertakers. Eventually it was agreed that the burial be completed later, and the rather embarrassed rector concluded the service with the coffin in an uncustomary position. Mr Parker of Balderton Hall (churchwarden) had to fetch Father back to enlarge the grave immediately after dispersal of the mourners.

The clay soil in the new churchyard posed problems when burials took place following a period of wet weather. Sometimes Father climbed down inside the grave to scoop out water lying in the bottom with a bowl-dish and bucket, before mourners arrived. The digging of a grave was tremendously heavy work, especially when the ground was soaked.

Upon Mr Wright's retirement, Father was asked by the rector to take over the position of sexton, which he did for many years. He was now kept busy on Sundays, attending all three services and ringing the bell/bells as appropriate. The working classes mainly attended the evening service, as farm work didn't cease on Sunday morning. The door to the belfry tower was to the right, below the unusual hexagonal-shaped church clock on the north side of the tower. This tower had been built in 1634 after the collapse of the old wooden steeple, and stonemason's marks dating from 1634 can still clearly be seen in the stonework.

Here Father gained access to the spiral staircase leading to the musty ringing chamber. He carefully locked the door from the inside for fear of being shut in. The rector's wife insisted that he do this, as a bell-ringer in her last parish had been locked in the tower for some time, and had repeatedly rung the bells until it was realised that all was not well. One of my greatest delights was to accompany Father when bell-ringing, especially on dark winter evenings when he carried our hurricane-lamp.

Nowadays the bells are rung from the Baptistry inside the church, so presumably village children no longer share in the excitement of climbing up into the belfry tower.

As sexton, Father was now responsible for cutting grass around the gravestones in the churchyard twice a year, for which a sum of 7/6d was paid upon delivery of a note to Mr Parker of Balderton, to the effect that the job was complete. We all helped with this task.

Very occasionally, families moved away from the village and Mother was asked to look after their family grave. This involved scrubbing the headstone for which 1/6d per year was sent by post, and I often assisted her.

Usually only very wealthy families could afford headstones in those days. Unless accurate parish records were kept at the time, many last resting-places of ordinary villagers will be forgotten forever.

When the Reverend Woolward retired, the Reverend Nesbitt followed. The groomsman was retained, as the new incumbent had five children, all of whom required transport to Yorton station each day to connect with trains to Wem or Whitchurch where they attended private schools.

Many villagers did not have the means of paying for an undertaker from Wem or Shrewsbury upon the death of a loved one. In these cases funerals were arranged by the church. Father, before he became sexton, was often asked to act as bearer, and for this purpose it was necessary for him to borrow a dark suit. A drink was provided at the inn for the bearers by the bereaved family, prior to the funeral, to give them the necessary strength. The six men then collected the bier from a lean-to outbuilding behind the church, and this they wheeled solemnly through the village. Everyone kept out of sight; curtains were pulled tight as a mark of respect. Sometimes the bearers would walk as far as Webscott, and then negotiate very awkward stairs at cottages, to bring the coffin down. It was then placed on the bier and pushed slowly to church for the service. Home-made wreaths and flowers were placed on the coffin, and mourners (dressed heavily in black) walked behind. One bell only was tolled at funerals.

Father was invited to be bearer many times, and when one of the others died, instructions were left that his dark suit should be passed on to Father. This was carefully brushed by Mother after use, folded, and then placed in a tin trunk and never used except for funerals. It was considered a great honour to be invited to bear a coffin and accompany an old friend on their last journey on this earth.

If someone was very ill, or dying, farmers used to lay sand on the lane outside the cottage, to soften the sound of wagons and horses. The metal rims of cart wheels were very noisy on the unsurfaced tracks.

Mrs Painter was usually called in for the 'laying-out'. She was greatly respected for this work among the bereaved, for which she dressed in black. The coffin-maker lived at Bomere Heath.

When Father became Sexton, Mother helped him in whatever way she could. She polished the pulpit and choir stalls, dusted the pews, and polished the altar brasses and rails.

CHAPTER FOURTEEN

Aunt Ethel

Aunt Ethel (one of Father's four sisters) was a person of quite remarkable individuality. I have mentioned in another chapter her work during WWI when she joined the Royal Flying Corps as an officer's bat-woman – responsible for officer's baggage on campaigns etc.

When hostilities ceased she was warmly welcomed back into the service of the titled lady for whom she worked in Ellesmere since leaving Myddle School. Much emphasis was placed in those days on service to one's country in time of war. Because of this and Ethel's devoted and trusted service over many years, she was quite unexpectedly rewarded, upon her mistress's death, by the then unbelievable sum of £500 in cash. This was a fortune in those days when farmworkers were paid 12/6d per week. Ethel also received, under the terms of the will, many antique items, valuable jewellery, silver, etc. All these treasures were also passed to her by Lady McCrutcheon.

One of my best recollections of Aunt Ethel is when she married. She announced, without warning, that she shortly intended to marry Thomas Husbands (a second village Lengthman to marry one of Father's sisters.) [A Lengthman was employed by the parish to repair and maintain the roads etc]. An atmosphere of overwhelming anticipation filled our normally sober household.

We three girls were quite beside ourselves with excitement, for this was our first-ever wedding invitation. Mother readily embarked on the ten mile walk to Wem and back, to procure pretty pink gingham for new frocks. She was soon busy at her sewing machine on the living-room table, singing happily, as three identical frocks took shape; and delightfully attractive they were, with big cape collars, enormous puffed sleeves and white lace trimmings.

Ethel married from her sister Alice's home, next door to us. Many villagers turned out to watch the arrival of the rector's coachman with horses and polished carriage to convey Aunt to church. Because of her new-found wealth, on a scale totally unknown in our family, Ethel was able to arrange a 'real' wedding with horses and carriage.

We walked excitedly to church with Mother, glancing frequently down at our new frocks. Uncle Jack Grice (Ethel's brother-in-law) gave her away, and she entered the church on his arm.

The excitement of the occasion enlivened his bronzed mischievous features, and Ethel was completely at ease. Mary Grice was Ethel's only bridesmaid. After the ceremony, we children threw the rice which had been in Mother's safekeeping, when Ethel emerged from the north door with her new husband. Her long hair was fastened neatly in a bun under a wide-brimmed blue hat. Her long fitted wedding dress was of blue-silk, with leg-of-mutton sleeves; several heavy gold bracelets adorned her wrists over her lacy gloves. The wedding breakfast which followed was held in Aunt Alice's parlour, an exceptionally attractive room with pretty window-blinds. We were given a generous portion of dainty food by aunt, and a small slice of wedding cake which she had made. This was one of the most happy days of our childhood, and there was much to discuss long after a rather 'merry' Father blew out our candle that night.

After her marriage Ethel moved into an estate cottage which she rented near Harmer Hill. Here all the priceless objects of her inheritance were displayed mainly on an antique oak table in her parlour. I loved to visit her with Mother just to see these treasures: little pieces of silver, china ornaments, pieces of porcelain and many other miscellaneous items. Children were never allowed to handle anything; aunt was very strict about this, as some were quite fragile.

The walls of aunt's kitchen were of crude bare sandstone, unrendered and unpainted, and consequently this room had a rather dark aspect. It was here that her newly-acquired mangle took pride of place. The sturdy object looked more like an apparatus for producing bank notes, than a mere laundry aid. In these days of spin dryers and automatic washing-machines, it is difficult to realise that aunt Ethel's mangle was regarded as a real luxury. Even a mangle was something which we could not afford; Mother's hands were always sore and red from wringing all our washing by hand.

On one particular visit to aunt Ethel, Mother and I were invited into the adjoining cottage by her neighbour, to see an infant who had died at 18 months. In those days people usually went to see the dead as an act of deference. Children were taken to view dead children, and death was accepted more openly.

Aunt Ethel and uncle Tom were very happily married for many years, aunt being an active and well-regarded member of the Women's Institute and a regular worshipper at the Parish Church. She had an eloquent voice and spoke with confidence. No doubt the experiences of her war work had influenced her general deportment.

CHAPTER FIFTEEN

Aunt Annie

Father's sister Annie was the only unmarried female remaining
in the family.

After leaving Myddle School, she was successful in
obtaining employment as a housekeeper with retired farmers.
She remained in this post until their demise. Annie worked hard
and was rewarded with the sum of £150 (a considerable amount
in those days) in their will. Annie was now 40.

Her next position was in Shrewsbury, but she later moved
to Birmingham. On the recommendation of the Shrewsbury
family she now worked for the owner of the White Swan Laundry
at Hunters Road, Handsworth.

Aunt became a regular worshipper at Handsworth Parish
Church (St Mary's) where, many years later, I was married myself
and my first child was baptised there. Aunt Annie was a supporter
of their amateur dramatic group. The church organised coach
tours – the driver being one of the churchwardens. The curate
always came to say a prayer on the coach before departure. She
visited Oberammergau in West Germany, near the Swiss border.
At Christmas short breaks were organised in the Cotswolds and

Aunt Annie also finished up in Birmingham, on one occasion visiting Oberammergau with the local church. After Helen married, Annie would frequently visit her and her family.

she took advantage of these.

Upon her retirement at sixty she was offered an alms house on Soho Road, Handsworth, by the church. They kindly gave her £50 to help buy furniture.

Aunt was of slim build, always smart in appearance, and never seen without a hat (summer and winter).

CHAPTER SIXTEEN

Beatrice (who died in infancy)
Mary (who died young)
Tom (who died scything) and others

When I was eleven years of age, Mother gave birth to a dear little baby girl, Beatrice, who sadly only survived for 14 months. She died in her pram following a convulsion whilst suffering from meningitis. Mrs Painter had been a tremendous help and comfort to Mother during the child's short illness.

It was a custom in our village, as a mark of respect, to visit the deceased. Thus schoolchildren, those who wanted to, came to see little Beatrice lying in her tiny coffin in the bedroom.

Funerals were simple affairs in those days, especially when they involved the burial of young children. Two little girls, Emily and Dolly, agreed to carry the small coffin from the cottage to church, Mother and Father followed, and we children walked slowly behind.

We had previously searched the old quarry, where people threw their rubbish, and had been successful in finding wire to frame into a wreath. This we covered with moss and filled with flowers from the garden and, with Mother's artistic touch, the effect was quite pleasing. This pretty garland lay on top of the coffin.

After a short funeral service, Beatrice was buried at grandfather's feet, under the slender leaning fir tree, near the lych gate. This old fir tree has witnessed the burial of three

A curious survival from Victorian times: a dog's grave from 1857 in the bluebell woods known as the Rector's Coppice, where generations of children have played. While the villagers were usually buried in unmarked graves, Sam, a Rector's pet dog, is commemorated by his own personal tombstone. Helen tells us there were at least three such graves.

members of my family beneath its shade. No stone marks their resting place.

We took a special pride in keeping our little sister's grave tidy, planting primroses and violets on the small grass mound. We kept the turf cut short and at Christmas we gathered berried holly and made a cross. This became an area of special significance for our family, under the fir tree in the peaceful churchyard.

Meanwhile, Mother posted funeral cards to notify distant relatives of the death. The envelopes were edged in black and the recipients knew instantly that they bore sad tidings.

*****

Mary Grice died at 19. She was my cousin, just six years older than me. Her parents, uncle Jack Grice and his wife Alice (my father's sister), were our neighbours for much of my childhood. They were eventually forced to move to a property on Myddle Hill at the time of the estate sale which had such an effect on all our lives.

A smile was never very far from Jack's bronzed face, nor a mischievous twinkle from his eye. He was the village lengthman, working on the lanes of the estate between a pair of red flags which marked the area of grass verge he was scything, and warned wagoners of his presence. His sister lived at Leyland in Lancashire, and during a visit to her, Jack remembered us three girls (as was his generous nature), and we were each presented upon his return with a pair of clogs. They were quite splendid – black leather, with a strap and large brass buckle. Uncle said they were the type worn by the mill girls and women in Lancashire at the time. We derived the greatest pleasure from wearing our new wooden-soled clogs as we never normally had any new clothes at all; these clogs were objects of interest and engaging curiosity for quite some time in the school playground.

Aunt Alice kept their cottage as neat as a pin. She had some pretty things and their home never seemed to be in the perpetual muddle ours was, with the chaos of so many of us in the small living room, with baby and pram in one corner. Mother made Alice's long aprons, always black for morning wear when dirty chores had to be done, and fresh white for the afternoon. Jack enjoyed an occasional pint of ale at the *Cross Keys* in the next village northwards, Burlton. Their son Jack did farm work and never married.

Poor Mary their daughter (born in 1905) was an intelligent girl, her parents having supplied books to encourage her reading, which was quite unusual in our family. On leaving school at 14 she went to work for Mr and Mrs Porch, as a maid, living in, as was the custom even though her home was so close. Mary was nicely dressed, well-spoken and participated in many church activities in what little free time she had. We were great friends, Mary and I; she took me to dances at Myddlewood Reading Room and sports days etc as her parents were not happy about her going alone.

Sadly, it was discovered that Mary had tuberculosis; she was sent to Sherlett Hospital near Ludlow but the treatment there was unsuccessful. She came home and spent most of her remaining days domiciled in a little wooden summer-house which Jack obtained when told there was not a great deal of hope. It was mounted on a turning mechanism, so that it could be moved away from the cold winds to which Myddle Hill was completely exposed, being the only high ground for many miles. She slept in this little garden house; there was no treatment, only fresh air; tuberculosis was common then and was usually regarded as incurable. Very few people went to visit Mary at this stage, as they were fearful of the disease. The young man to whom she had become engaged regularly called, right up to the end. Mother continued to visit, but would stand and talk from a distance.

Mary had a favourite and much treasured little book, given her by Aunt Ethel, and she instructed her mother that, upon her death, the book should be passed to my sister Dorothy (being the youngest in the family). In turn, Dorothy always treasured the book, and it remained in our family – consisting of a poem by Wordsworth with one verse on each page and beautiful illustrations, the verses written between delicate drawings of wild flowers. It always had great significance for us, being a family of seven children of whom one was buried by the churchyard tree after dying in infancy.

Mary often read this poem while imprisoned in her summer-house; possibly it helped her approach her death with fortitude.

She died at 19 and it was the greatest loss our family had known, for everyone loved Mary. Her untimely death was difficult for her parents to accept.

I learned much of the poem by heart, and in later years recited it to my own children. I always thought it was one of the most beautiful poems I had ever read: encompassing life and death of children.

We Are Seven

I met a little cottage girl,
She was eight years old, she said.
Her hair was thick with many a curl
That clustered round her head.

She had a rustic, woodland air
And she was wildly clad;
Her eyes were fair, and very fair;
Her beauty made me glad.

'Sisters and brothers, little Maid,
How many may you be?'
'How many? Seven in all' she said,
And wondering, looked at me.

'And where are they? I pray you tell.'
She answered, 'Seven are we;
And two of us at Conway dwell,
And two are gone to sea.

Two of us in the churchyard lie,
My sister and my brother;
And in the churchyard cottage, I
Dwell near them with my mother.'

'You say that two at Conway dwell,
And two are gone to sea,
Yet ye are seven! I pray you tell,
Sweet Maid, how this may be.'

Then did the little maid reply,
'Seven boys and girls are we:
Two of us in the churchyard lie
Beneath the churchyard tree.'

'You run about, my little Maid,
Your limbs they are alive;
If two are in the churchyard laid,
Then ye are only five.'

'Their graves are green, they may be seen,'
The little Maid replied,
'Twelve steps or more from my mother's door
And they are side by side.

My stockings there I often knit,
My kerchief there I hem;
And there upon the ground I sit,
And sing a song to them.

And often after sunset, sir,
When it is light and fair,
I take my little porringer,
And eat my supper there.

The first that died was sister Jane;
In bed she moaning lay,
Till God released her of her pain;
And then she went away.

So in the churchyard she was laid;
And, when the grass was dry,
Together round her grave we played,
My brother John and I.

And when the ground was white with snow,
And I could run and slide,
My brother John was forced to go,
And he lies by her side.'

'How many are you, then,' said I,
If they two are in heaven?'
Quick was the little maid's reply,
'O Master! we are seven.'

'But they are dead; those two are dead!
Their spirits are in heaven!'
'Twas throwing words away; for still
The little Maid would have her will,
And said, 'Nay, we are seven!'

William Wordsworth (1798)

Mary was one of the first to be buried in the churchyard extension. There was controversy at the time over this addition, older inhabitants expressing opinions that they had no wish to be buried in this new area but preferred the old churchyard. But when the extension was opened and the land consecrated, it gradually became accepted.

Mary, her brother Jack, aunt Alice and uncle Jack all lie here, in unmarked graves, alongside the south wall, near the commencement of a footpath to Myddle Park.

*****

A TRAGIC LUNCHTIME DEATH

Deaths on the unmetalled lanes were more common in the horse-and-cart era than is generally realised. A tragic death which happened just around the corner on Myddle Bank stunned the whole village. It was the accidental death of Harry, the popular head wagoner at Castle Farm. The fatal accident occurred around harvest time when he had been employed cutting corn with a binder.

On this fateful day he came down Myddle Bank at lunchtime. Two horses were pulling the binder; Harry leading them. Something startled the animals at the bend, they reared up in fright and crushed poor Harry. The horses ran out of control, racing through the main street, binder in tow, until coming to a halt in the yard at Castle Farm. Mother saw the horses and went out to see what had happened; she found poor Harry lying on the bank in a pool of blood. Marjorie's mother was immediately sent for, she could always be relied upon to give first-aid or advice in any kind of emergency. The dear man's brains were scattered over the bank and Mrs Painter knew as soon as she saw the gaping hole in his head, that there was no hope for him. Another neighbour had hurried to the school, to ask Mr Porch to keep the children indoors, until the bank was cleared. Luckily no-one else was hurt by the horses and binder, another few minutes and there might have been disastrous consequences as children would have been coming out of school.

This accident was particularly poignant as Harry spent all his working days with horses and they were his livelihood. Mother was asked to attend the Inquest. This was held at Baschurch Public Hall and her expenses of 1/6d were paid for attending.

This kind of gruesome death could occur when horses hauling wagons and carts went out of control. Another such incident from the previous century is recorded briefly but memorably on a tombstone on the outside wall of Petton Church (just outside the parish), thus:

In Memory of Edwd Hayward Whose Death
was caused by the Wheels of a Waggon
Going over his Head
on the 3rd September 18(??) [date unreadable]

******

Deaths of farm animals could sometimes be almost as harrowing for us as human deaths. In particular I always remember the slaughter at Alford Farm during an outbreak of foot-and-mouth disease in about 1922. We played often with the children at Alford Farm.

The farmer here discovered that his cattle were diseased and the animals would have to be destroyed. Volunteers for this work were sought in the village; the entire stock was killed. Shots could be heard reverberating for most of the day, and the atmosphere in our cottage was one of great sadness, as we all loved the animals. We were well aware that the farmer would face severe hardship, as there was no compensation in those days. There was not a smile on anyone's face in the village that day.

TOM (WHO DIED SCYTHING)

Uncle Tom, who had rescued sister Elsie from our dirty drain, sadly collapsed and died while scything their large garden. His body lay out of doors all night and was not discovered until the following day. He was still clutching the scythe which had to be cut away from his hand. Searches for him had taken place at Harmer Hill and Myddle, and enquiries made of neighbours and family. He had, unknown to Aunt Ethel, been working in an uncultivated and wildly overgrown area of their large garden when death struck. Aunt had married relatively late in life, in her 30's, and they had no children.

Tom's brother, William Husbands, was killed in WWI serving in France.

After moving to Myddle Hill as a consequence of the estate sale, uncle Jack (Grice) enjoyed spending warm summer evenings, smoking his pipe sitting on the wide sandstone wall, opposite his new abode. This is at a point where a footpath commences which crossed the fields to Houlston and the Witterage.

The sandstone wall was fairly long and Uncle Jack told us children, that he had heard that the reason the wall was in that position, was that when folk had stolen sheep or cattle, they were criminals.

Consequently they were taken up to this wall and shot, as they were not fit to live in the village. They were then rolled in a winding sheet and buried under the wall. This may or may not be an authentic tale but it gives a reason for such a substantial wall being built at this odd spot.

CHAPTER SEVENTEEN

'Gipsy' Baker's Merrington Mission

The wild exposed area known as Merrington Green was 400ft above sea level and some 50ft higher than the countryside around it. This unlikely location witnessed one of the greatest religious revivals ever known in Shropshire.

Commoners possessed ancient grazing rights, and grazing over the centuries had produced good-quality grassland. The Green was the scene of one of the largest gipsy encampments in north Shropshire; at times between 20 and 30 vans were visible, standing high and imposing off the ground on enormous painted wheels. Wagon horses grazed freely on the heathland of 30 acres or so, as did cattle and goats. Each year, at Easter, the gipsies converged on the Green for a general celebration, which included a ram roast. They journeyed long distances to participate. This brought heavier than usual wagon traffic through Myddle; as one can imagine, the sight was quite spectacular.

Some of the wagons which ambled through on the way to Merrington were so heavy that two horses were required to pull hard at the shafts. They often took on water at the pump. Because of the steepness of the Bank, we were privileged that the wagons passed our cottage, taking the more gentle route to the top highway. My sisters and I regularly took up positions on our doorstep to witness the quite remarkable sight. Sometimes we ran to our bedroom window from where we had a splendid view right inside. Rarely we would see a decorated wagon embellished with gold scrolls and flowers, but more commonly the colour was plain 'gipsy' maroon with gold wheels. Bow or square-top wagons were a frequent sight; some wagons were tall, with clerestory windows in the roof; yet others were more impoverished and could only be described as covered canvas wagons. We saw many horse-traders, with two or maybe three horses tied to the back of the vehicles. The dark-complexioned womenfolk and children walked up the steep bank and waited on Myddle Hill for their menfolk to take the wagons round.

These women at times hawked from door to door, carrying their wares in a basket – reels of black or white cotton, lace, pegs, boot laces, etc. This trading was by no means one-way; quantities of our rhubarb were regularly purchased by them.

Upon misbehaving, father's strict threat to the miscreant child was that he or she would be sold to the gipsies; but these warnings never quite had the desired effect, as we all thought the gipsies' nomadic way of life exciting and appealing. In fact we envied them, and welcomed the prospect of joining these mysterious travelling people!

Mother took us for a rare picnic on the Green one summer; we didn't venture too close to the encampment, but were interested in a squatter's hut which we observed with curiosity in passing. The framework consisted of two iron bedsteads (one at each end) with poles and sacking making up the sides. A very crude thatching job had been executed on the roof in an effort to drain off rainwater; the hut had been constructed close to the hedge for shelter and we could see an old oil stove, which was obviously used for heating. It was hard for us children to imagine a man living in these conditions; he was the only squatter on the Green at the time but Mother could remember others who had lived in similar abodes. This particular man, who was not at home on the day of our visit, was a dealer in rabbit-skins and sometimes called at the village.

Other visitors by horse-drawn caravan (apart from gipsies) were two uniformed sisters of the Church Army, taking part in a crusade against alcoholism, which (as we shall see) could have devastating effects on poor families. The wagon, which they courageously drove, bore religious texts, and inside were small tables festooned with literature they were distributing. At appointed times the sisters delivered talks – many people went to listen. They attended the services at the Parish Church on Sundays, the Rector allowing them to put the caravan and horse into his field. This was opposite the Rectory and much later was sold for council housing, the rather agreeable development being named 'The Glebelands'.

Also from time to time the paraffin seller from Wem rumbled slowly through in a pointed-topped canvas-covered wagon, which was always an interesting sight. (Paraffin was later sold in the granary of the store).

Another not infrequent trader was Mr Burrows of Wem, with his odd two-wheel horse-drawn cart. His occupation was rather macabre in that he dealt in animal flesh and collected dead horses, cattle, etc from the farms. The corpses were covered over with a black sheet. His business advertised regularly in the *Wellington Journal* and I quote below such an advertisement which appeared much earlier (in 1902), when the Journal cost 1d.

E. BURROWS, High Street, Wem
Having secured order for supplying the
Shropshire Hunt Kennels with flesh for
the hounds, is prepared to give best
prices for dead or worn out horses,
cows and will remove them wholesale
within 10 miles of Wem.

Prompt cash before removal. Telegrams paid for.

To return to the Pentecostal missionary, Pastor John Wesley Baker. Well-known locally as 'Gipsy Baker' because of his work among the gipsy families (although he was not a gipsy), was a familiar figure to be seen cycling through Myddle on his way to prayer meetings in Ellesmere. Always smart in appearance, he dressed in a black suit and black boots. A wide-brimmed black felt hat shaded his kindly eyes, the brim pinned to his collar by two large safety-pins to prevent the hat blowing off as he rode along. His hair was white and shoulder-length, and he had a smile and greeting for everyone.

Pastor Baker was another inhabitant of Merrington Green, where he dwelled in the living-section of his self-built mission chapel. He was a man who was greatly respected by the inhabitants of Merrington, who attended his services along with the gipsies who camped on the green, and others who walked or cycled many miles to prayer meetings.

Word reached us, via the school playground, that he possessed a talking parrot which was said to perch on his pulpit during Sunday afternoon gospel services, usually attended by children with their parents. It was even said that the parrot could sing and join in choruses.

From a combination of curiosity as to what a parrot actually looked like, and to verify the truth of the rumour that a bird could actually sing 'human words', we obtained our parents' consent to attend an afternoon service at the Merrington Mission. We set off with friend Marjorie.

We covered numerous miles on foot as children and always felt safe on the lanes.

John Wesley 'Gipsy' Baker with his dog. A court case ensued after unruly children tied a tin can to the dog's tail!

THE

Pentecostal Witness

Glad Tidings

FROM

THE MERRINGTON MISSION.

"And they were all filled with the Holy Ghost and began to speak with other tongues."—*Acts ii. 4.*
"I would that ye all spake with tongues."—*[St. Paul].*
—*I Cor. xiv. 5.*

"I thank my God, I speak with tongues more than ye all."—*I Cor. xiv. 18.*
"Though it tarry, wait for it, because it will surely come."—*Habakkuk ii. 3.*

Edited by THEOPHILUS TREVOR.

No. 3.   MARCH, 1909.   Price One Penny.

"He hath made of one blood all nations of men"—*Acts xvii. 26.*

'Tis the very same power
That they had at Pentecost,
'Tis the power, Jesus promised
Should come down.

It was while they all were praying,
And believing it would come,
Came the power, Jesus promised
Should come down.

'Tis the very same power
For I feel it in my soul,
'Tis the power, Jesus promised
Should come down.

"The Blood of Jesus Christ, God's Son, cleanseth us from all Sin."—*I John, i, 7.*

Above: A church specially designed for people who didn't like going inside buildings? In 1909 this picture of the 'Gypsy Mission Tent' adorned the front cover of 'Pentecostal Witness' (Merrington Mission's monthly magazine), which circulated over much of Shropshire. The solid-looking doorway would suggest that the structure was intended to stay in one place for some time; Merrington Green was then a semi-permanent encampment where gipsies would call for short periods of their travels, giving evangelists such as 'Gipsy' Baker (in reality not a gipsy at all) the opportunity to preach the gospel to people who normally had no occasion to hear it, and perhaps would not have readily gone inside a church anyway.

The only object we were fearful of meeting was a bull!

We knew the pastor was fond of animals as he had taken two young men to court for tying a tin can to his dog's tail, and terrifying the poor animal. (They were each fined one shilling for the offence, and Mr Baker took the tin to court for people to see). Marjorie thought the goats on the Green were also his.

As we climbed the gradual gradient from Merrington, distant palls of wood-smoke became visible above the trees, signifying the presence of the encampment. The walk had taken longer than we anticipated and we found the chapel, which lay some way back from the lane, surprisingly full. We had no option but to stand at the rear and other late-comers stood outside. Many of the gipsy women present wore long silk frocks, with a scarf tied loosely around their dark hair. Their children too were very smart, and some little girls had necklaces of amber beads. The congregation before us were quietly seated and we could see across to the pulpit over the heads and voluminous hats, worn by women from nearby hamlets.

Sure enough, there was the parrot we had walked so far to see, his grey claws clinging tightly to his perch: this was quite the most beautiful bird we had ever seen! His tiny eyes surveyed the large congregation. Eventually, the bird did join in the singing of some of the more familiar children's hymns, to our immense delight.

Our next opportunity to walk to Merrington to take another look at the intriguing bird was on a Wednesday. No sooner had we opened the chapel door, than it started screeching, 'It's not Sunday! It's not Sunday!' We ran!

Before the chapel was built, a huge 'Gipsy Mission Tent' had previously stood on the same site, provided by the Pentecostal Church. A gipsy wagon had stood alongside, providing living accommodation for pastor Baker. The pastor had travelled to different places before the tent was pitched on Merrington Green, and had preached to anyone who attended the meetings, not only gipsies.

In 1909 Pastor Baker began producing a magazine called *The Pentecostal Witness*, edited by one Theophilus Trevor. It is interesting to read of people travelling from many parts of the county to the tent at Merrington. Most of the information on the following pages has been taken from copies of *The Pentecostal Witness* of 1909:

'*The mission spread throughout North Shropshire. At Wollerton, there was great local interest and the congregation which gathered there for the opening service quite surpassed all expectations.*

Picklescote saw great crowds at the opening service there. This village, three miles north of Long Mynd, is often described as the Shropshire Alps, because of its situation 973ft above sea level; but not too high for people to live there in the farmsteads and cottages dotted about hill and dale.

The Ellesmere branch of the Pentecostal Mission began humbly in two cottages, one in the centre of the town, the other situated on the outskirts, in a district known locally as The Cross. In both places, John Wesley Baker brought people to God, for the people there began to get sober, saved and filled with the Spirit.

At Affcot, near Craven Arms, large congregations were present at the Primitive Methodist Chapel, Leamoor Common, on Christmas Day. The evening service, of three hours, was conducted by Mr Wesley Baker. The Sunday after Christmas, Mr Wm Jones offered his house at Affcot, situated on the old west coast road, for the continuation of the mission.

Members of the Merrington Mission were invited to speak at the little Primitive Methodist Chapel at Weston. Word having spread how God had blessed the mission, the Chapel was filled to capacity.

And so the Mission spread. In the Primitive Methodist Chapel at Pontesbury, John Wesley Baker gave an impressive address on '*The lost sheep, the lost silver and the lost son*'. *The great crowd of people were loth to disperse and after the benediction had been pronounced, they would not go and the meeting continued until well-nigh midnight, after which members of the congregation had to bravely march through the blinding January snow, in some cases miles to their homes.*

Easter meetings at the old tent began with the early morning prayer meeting at 5am which lasted until 8.30am. It is recorded that two young men cycled 25 miles, and another walked 10 miles, in order to be at the prayer meeting at the specified time. A baptismal service was held in the afternoon; the place chosen was four miles away at Mytton, in the river Perry. The natural beauty of this sequestered spot, and the gentle flow of the stream, made it an ideal baptismal font. A great meeting was held at the tent that night and many could not gain admittance. Members of several different sections were present at this meeting, both Anglicans and Nonconformists, people from different parts of the county and distant provincial towns. (According to the Witness those who spoke at this meeting included 'Messrs Rawson and Jones, Mrs Wood, Mrs Mansell, the Misses Delbridge, Miss Alice Stephens, Miss Edwards and Mrs Trevor.')

An open-air meeting took place in the delightful 'health resort' of Church Stretton whilst the Annual Fair was in progress. A large number of people were attracted and attentively listened to the songs and testimonies given. Craven Arms and several other places were visited with encouraging results.

The mission work was entirely self-supporting and relied on subscriptions from friends and supporters, with a system of collecting boxes and cards. Such was the authentic flavour of religious fervour at the turn of the century, donations were published in the magazine, together with comments which might accompany them.'

Alcoholism was one of the greatest social problems of the time which caused much anguish to Mr Baker, and this was a theme taken up by the mission.

One Will Davies, who lived on the Green next door to Marjorie's brother Dick, was a heavy drinker. On pay day he would go into inns and spend most of his wages on drink, bringing home 2/6d for his wife Lizzie to keep house with. He was persuaded to attend a service at the tent by Mrs Emily Buckley, a gipsy from the nearby encampment, a woman who had been converted and now led others to Christ. It was then through the teachings of pastor Baker that his life was changed after being converted and baptised in the River Perry by him. He remained a deeply religious man.

Pastor Baker's following proved so great that when the appointed time arrived for him to move with the tent to a new mission field in 1920/21, he asked if he might be permitted to stay. It was agreed by the Pentecostal Church that he could remain, but would have to forfeit the tent, which was now needed elsewhere. That was how the existing chapel came to be built by John Wesley Baker, with the help of his nephew Frank Baker and other volunteers who were only too pleased to assist with the construction of a permanent place of worship. The timbers for the chapel (made of timber and corrugated-iron) came via Old Woods railway sidings, then by horse and cart to the site. The collapsible seats and matting he was allowed to retain, but he lost his secretary, who had been paid until then by the church. The new chapel was financed by Pastor Baker, who owned it when completed. He never married.

His following was quite overwhelming over the next few years. Dick Painter's daughter Gwen was often taken over to the chapel as a child by her neighbour Will Davies. She recalls Mr Baker teaching her recitations in the form of religious poems, which she was required to learn for Sunday School. While there she was given rice pudding which he had cooked in a large black iron pot, on top of a coal-fired stove. On warm summer evenings she joined him for tea, out of doors, under a hedge on the Green, where, at a small table covered with a spotless white tablecloth, they ate strawberries and cream together (first going to his garden to pick the strawberries).

Her last memory of John Wesley Baker was when Mr Will Davies called her mother on a Good Friday morning to assist him, after finding Mr Baker collapsed on the floor, having suffered a stroke. She watched as he left the mission chapel for the last time, carried away down the narrow cinder path on a stretcher, with his outstanding white curly hair clearly visible in the morning sunshine, to the road and the waiting ambulance. He was taken to the Royal Salop Infirmary where later he died. The year would be about 1940.

This remarkable Pentecostal evangelist is, according to local people, buried in an unmarked grave somewhere in nearby

Pastor Baker later built this 'chapel' of timber and corrugated-iron, where Helen heard his parrot quoting chunks of hymns at children's services. He certainly knew how to entertain a young congregation! Baker died in 1940 and gipsies come to Merrington no more, but the 'chapel' still stood in the 1980s, now hedged in and used as a private residence.

Preston Gubbals churchyard. His life's work was to acquaint all people, whether poorly-paid agricultural workers, gipsies, gamblers, squatters, alcoholics or whoever, with the love of God through the gospels. He was respected by everyone, especially the gipsies with whom he lived. He worked for over 30 years from his base at the Gipsy Mission Tent and then the Merrington Mission Chapel, and converted many thousands, bringing about a great revival of religion in the area.

His early convert, Mr Will Davies, remained one of his last friends, and continued services in the chapel after the pastor's death, until it was eventually sold. The seats were given to the Methodist Chapel at Walford Heath.

All that remains today to remind us of this revolutionary pastor, is the old lichen-encrusted chapel which he built, now a private residence.

CHAPTER EIGHTEEN

Jessie's House in the Rock, and Webscott

The pretty wooded hamlet of Webscott lay between brook and high cliffs, and straddled the north side of the Lower Road. Quaint sandstone cottages lay dotted under the hillside, in the lee of a steep rock outcrop. Many had hand-laid cobble paths and yards, the stones coming from the fields lying to the south when these had been cleared for farmers by women and children, forced by circumstance to earn a few pence in this laborious way, a generation earlier.

New development has not, as yet, spoiled the Lower Road as in Myddle, where the building boom has resulted in modern houses and bungalows being carelessly shoe-horned into every vacant corner of the historic village. Changes are beginning to take place however; the idyllic stone cottage where Doris Watkins lived, and wild-flowing periwinkle obscured the two noble stone gateposts, has sadly joined the list of outstanding properties now demolished. New modern homes are appearing beneath the hill. Few visitors can imagine the rustic building delights of a bygone age which still await them at the further reaches of the Lower Road.

The architectural gem known as 'The Nest' could not avoid making a breathtaking impact upon a stranger. Standing magnificently on a high bank of rock above the lane, it elegantly dominated this attractive wooded corner. Its western facing walls made use of the actual rock face. This beautifully proportioned house boasted a fine display of diamond lattice windows, bearing a strong resemblance to those at the *Red Lion* inn. My route when delivering telegrams after school to the Reverend Lewis, a retired clergyman, lay up a steep well-worn flight of steps, hewn through the soft red sandstone bank, which was the access for pedestrians from the lane. An unexpected overhead footbridge spanned the steps, apparently bridging two sections of the Reverend Lewis' delightful garden. The impressive stone porch and weathered oak door faced south. The rear of this building was devoid of sunlight with steep perpendicular cliffs rising protectively to shelter it. Here and there a wind-blown pine struggled to find a foothold in the crag above the house.

The hamlet possessed the additional attraction of providing the only alternative store within easy walking distance of the village; albeit a small business occupying the front parlour of one of the distinctive cottages. If Marjorie's mother gave her a few pennies to spend on sweets, and we were free of duties for a while, we walked, with other children, to Webscott. The shopkeeper was Mr Owen, a corpulent red-faced man, in neat white apron, with an enormous purple nose. It was no secret that his nose proved an irreverent attraction, particularly to boys from our village. He extended an enthusiastic welcome as we crowded into his little establishment, as customers were infrequent in a hamlet the size of Webscott, and much valued, even children from the neighbouring village with only pennies to spend between them, and all morning in which to do it!

When we were young the quarries at Webscott were still worked, and provided employment for men from the village. We watched with great interest, as slabs of sandstone, which were our local geology, were cut from the hillside. These were then manoeuvered, with the aid of ropes and much difficulty, onto a long dray. Two great wagon horses delivered the heavy consignment to the Estate Depot yard at Myddlewood, where it was stored for building and repair purposes.

Where the sandstone had been removed, the scarring of the hillside had the effect of making extraordinary giant staircases, their enormous steps leading away up to the summit. The closest chapel to the village was located at Webscott; the neat stone memorial plaque over the door read '1842 Primitive Methodist Chapel'. The simply-built stone chapel stood at the wayside in Merrington Lane. The building was minute, but carefully constructed by an anonymous local craftsman who paid much attention to detail, as is evidenced by the decorative edging stone under the eaves, following the pitch of the roof.

In the 1980s, this dear little Methodist chapel, its windows and door sealed with rusting sheets of corrugated metal, is used to store sacks of fertiliser.

*****

Sunday School existed at the time for children who lived near. Mr Bourne, who ran our store, was often invited to preach. I infrequently accompanied Mother to evening worship, and it was obvious to all that Mr Bourne simply repeated that morning's sermon from the Parish Church, while it was still fresh in his mind! So the Rector's words reached a wider congregation than he realised! Field footpaths were used by worshippers in dry weather, and provided a very agreeable alternative walk from Myddle.

Free churches were not allowed to build within one mile of the Parish Church in those days. The interesting network of field paths interlacing the parish were much used by farm workers to reach their places of employment, pedlars, and in fine weather churchgoers, before lanes were properly surfaced. The advantage of these routes was their directness and in many instances the distance by the lanes was halved.

Myddle's last working blacksmith, Mr Albert Neale, lived at Webscott until his death at 88 years; he is buried in Myddle churchyard. His birthplace was Forden, near Welshpool, on 10 October 1882. Setting up as a blacksmith for a while at Brook Cottage, Webscott, he moved his trade in 1925 to Myddle

Smithy. Mrs Florence Neale, his widow, continued living at Brook Cottage until 1988, when she was forced to move due to ill-health to a nursing home near Whitchurch, where she lived until she reached 100 years.

Brook Cottage was a compelling old sandstone dwelling situated on the corner at the junction of Lower Road and Merrington Lane. Neat cobbled paths circumvented the building, and the pretty garden extended alongside the brook. The delightful old-fashioned living-room possessed an imposing corner-mounted range, which concentrated one's loitering gaze by its eccentricity. A collection of forged iron hearth furniture: poker, tongs and the like, lay against the fender, all clean and inky black. A not altogether unexpected collection of ornate iron horseshoes adorned mantel and shelves; delicate filigree work interlacing the shoes which Mr Neale, a master-craftsman, had designed and forged over the years, to commemorate special occasions and family anniversaries.

This cottage was deceptively large; as well as a separate kitchen, a snug little parlour led off the living room and shared a corner chimney with the range next-door. The covers on the sofa cushions had been meticulously hand-embroidered in art silks and depicted crinoline-dressed ladies carrying parasols, in country cottage scenes. The bedrooms were upstairs. The interior of the cottage was homely and warm and the peace therein only invaded by the constant questioning calls of doves and pigeons nesting in the nearby escarpment. The site was encompassed by a solid stone wall with extravagant stone gateposts, a bonus from earlier days when the sympathetic builder-cum-stonemason could afford to be unrestrained in his use of sandstone.

Our school friend Jessie also lived at Webscott at an unbelievably secluded hideout. It was discovered by leaving the lane, ascending a steep bank, and turning sharp left, behind the screen of stone. This cottage, concealed from the world, was built against the flat-rock face, where years earlier the sandstone had been quarried. The rooms which employed the rock for a wall

By Helen's later years, Webscott Chapel (1842) was in a bad state *(above and below)* seemingly abandoned or used as a farm storage building – with rough wooden doors, and windows on one side replaced by sheets of corrugated-iron. Myddle village itself never had a non-conformist chapel. In Helen's day Webscott chapel, tiny as it was, had a regular congregation which packed its small space. Helen occasionally attended with her mother.

were chilly and damp, according to my sister Dorothy who had visited the secret dwelling.

Jessie's were a delightfully old-fashioned family who dressed in a quaint Victorian manner. For all important village occasions her father sported an outsize black jacket, with huge orange checks and a neat black velvet collar. A tall bowler hat, with tiny brim, accompanied the outfit, as did a curious pair of breeches, just to his knees. Her quiet mother dressed in a black cape in winter and wore a flat-topped black hat. An odd fur contrivance fastened under the chin and covered the front part of her body. I cannot say what this was called, or if women wore these things in the towns: certainly no-one else in our village had one. It was no doubt practical and protected her chest from the cold winds, which in this part of Shropshire could be very cold indeed. Her hands stayed inside a warm fur muff, both summer and winter, except when sliding out to wave to people they passed on their journeys by donkey cart. This again was unusual, and they were the only family to possess one. It was like a home-made box, with a wide board placed across to form a seat. The three

Not far from Webscott was the 'House in the Rock', whence Jessie King, her chest sometimes protected by fatty bacon rashers, came to school over 90 years ago. The house subsequently fell into ruin, but was later rebuilt from the original sandstone blocks; the rear and side walls were the rock-face itself.

squashed inside the little cart with difficulty, father overflowing it somewhat due to his bulky build. This odd form of transport was used whenever they ventured out; the family clambering from the cart when an incline was encountered to ease the load on the donkey. They were a friendly, sincere family who actively involved themselves in all local events and were much respected in the area.

Jessie had lovely yellow hair which her mother plaited down to her waist, brown shining eyes, and a wicked little smile on her face that made her look the happiest child on earth – and who knows, perhaps she was. Jessie also had the benefit of the family's ante-diluvian 'dress-code'. Her knickers were hand-made with a band at the waist and an opening at each side, fastening with four linen buttons, which were always falling off. We were all-too-familiar with Jessie's undergarments because of the regularity with which we assisted her stitching back fallen buttons; this being done in the privacy of the smelly school toilets, with needle and cotton provided by Mrs Porch. Her bright red flannel petticoat tied at the back of her neck, so as to keep her chest warm; this too was most beautifully hand-sewn.

When one day she came to school and said she had bacon stitched inside her chemise we just didn't believe her, so she pulled up her dress to show us, and sure enough, her mother had secured pieces of fatty bacon across her chest to protect her from the cold. Some mothers rubbed their children's chests with goose oil in wintertime, but we didn't get this kind of treatment.

Jessie was habitually dressed in a lovely black linen frock, the skirt of which was a series of frills. I think her mother stitched another frill on to the bottom as Jessie grew, because all the time we knew her she only wore this type of black frock. Her legs were kept warm by black hand-knitted stockings and button-up boots. On top of her black dress went a long black coat, then came a hand-knitted bonnet and large black fur muff. She was a delightful child, with a distinctive personal character, who helped enormously to brighten dull days at Myddle school.

She surprised us all when she came to school one day and said she was going to live in Canada, then followed a note for Mr Porch saying that she and her parents were sailing for Canada in March.

She wrote a long letter to the school in October, telling of the voyage and adding that the part of Canada where they were living might be snowed up for Christmas, and they wouldn't be able to get out for weeks. Then she wrote again at Christmas, but we never heard from her after that, although she was often in our thoughts. What became of their donkey cart I never knew, but I certainly haven't seen anything like it since.

CHAPTER NINETEEN

The Old Trades:
Blacksmith, Carrier, Saddler and
Tree-feller, Farrier and Wheelwright

I grew up at a time when motor transport was beginning to penetrate remote villages for the first time.

Petrol cars and buses had become quite common in the big cities years before I was born. But small villages like Myddle, far from the main centres of industry, were at first little affected by the huge changes brought about by the petrol engine.

When I was a girl and until the middle 1920s, the horse continued to provide the basic motive-power for most people's journeys; while poorer people and their children inevitably did little travelling. Until I was 17 I never went more than 10 miles from my own village except for a once-only outing to the seaside. I rarely even went to Shrewsbury. I never went to London at all until my daughter took me in later life. Travel was simply not a normal part of an ordinary person's life.

Obviously people who stayed most of the time in their own villages were far more dependent than nowadays on the variety of tradespeople which the countryside used to support. There was never much money about, but what little there was, was all spent in Myddle. Because of this, small villages at that time supported a variety of tradespeople whose successors nowadays usually work in nearby towns – and provide services for people forced to travel into the towns because they can no longer get what they want in the villages.

Public transport didn't penetrate our village until I was about ten, when a petrol-bus service began. It operated twice weekly on Wednesdays (one return bus) and Saturdays (three buses) between Shrewsbury and Myddle, buses turning in the inn yard and taking on passengers at the store. Later the service was extended to serve Ellesmere, and when this happened, passengers often left cycles and prams in our wash-house, as our cottage then became the bus stop for the village.

Before this service started, villagers had no alternative other than to hire Mr Mullinux of Myddlewood and his dray, if circumstances warranted a journey away from home. But this was a very rare occurrence for the average cottage-dweller.

Mr Mullinux lived in an unusual (albeit imposing) house built after the style of the London and North Western Railway, in grey brick with corners embellished in yellow brick, with a slate roof and tall ornamental chimneys.

He was called upon in emergencies, like the time when my uncle Jack Grice (who lived next door to us) was taken ill. Aunt Alice's linseed poultices were not helping him, and the doctor confirmed that uncle had pneumonia and must be taken to the Infirmary immediately. A lad was despatched in haste off to Myddlewood for Mr Mullinux, who first had to catch the horse in the field and harness it. Poor uncle Jack was carried from the cottage by neighbours, wrapped in blankets and placed high between Mr Mullinux and Jack (junior) my cousin. No-one else could go because of the additional weight which might slow down the horse.

Mr Mullinux returned very late, with the little candle lamp shining on the dray, Uncle Jack being safely in a bed at the Royal Salop Infirmary. Thereafter, he took Aunt Alice, Mary (their daughter) and Jack (it was a tight squeeze) weekly on Sunday afternoons to visit, for about three weeks, until uncle was sufficiently recovered to be brought home.

Mr Porch, the schoolmaster, and his wife (also a teacher) often hired the dray for transporting themselves and their baggage to Yorton station. In wet weather, one just opened up an umbrella. This service was invaluable to the community in emergencies. On Saturdays Mr & Mrs Mullinux provided a trading service, taking goods (mostly home-grown produce and eggs) to sell at Shrewsbury market for villagers. They brought specific items back if requested to do so. Mother occasionally ordered two-penny-worth of iodine from the chemists, which was the panacea for all things in those days. Some of the farmers' children sent for raffia, which they made into little table-mats, mainly to place under oil lamps.

Later an enterprising smallholder, one Lloyd Owen of Marton, began a regular service from the village into Shrewsbury. He owned a cattle truck with canvas sides, into which he placed loose bench seats. This service operated on Saturdays only, leaving Myddle at 5pm and returning at 11pm – the shops in the town remained open until about 10pm in those days and many people took advantage of the opportunity to get to Shrewsbury. The fare was 1/6d return. Some people preferred evening shopping as it took them away from their oil-lit cottages into the bright lights of a town, although the means of transport was pretty uncomfortable by modern standards. (Our family could not use this service as the fare was too high.)

In these days of a 15-minute car journey into Shrewsbury, it is almost impossible to imagine living in a village where the only regular transport consisted of the various bone-shaking carts and other vehicles which I have described.

Having two railway stations relatively close at hand (Yorton 2 miles and Baschurch 3 miles) hardly helped families who never really had enough money to pay a rail-fare. Not that railway-fares were particularly high; but our finances simply did not leave money to spare for luxuries such as rail journeys. We could not even afford new clothes. For much of this period all our spare money had to go towards paying for the house.

Baschurch Station, on the Great Western Railway main line between Shrewsbury and Chester, was of course an important place in the locality, even though I never boarded a train there until I was 17. Most farm produce went away by rail in those days, and many supplies reached Myddle via the Baschurch goods yard. The station possessed a fine conglomeration of buildings and substantial goods yard. It had been opened in 1848 by the Shrewsbury and Chester Railway. The buildings were of an ornate cottage design with elaborately carved barge-boards. An attractive sandstone water-tower with slate roof and finial stood west of the main station building, and next to this was the station master's house. There were large goods sidings from which cattle were transported, and a coal merchant's office. A tall wooden signal-box stood near the roadside level crossing gate.

There was an unfortunate accident at this station when I was still a schoolgirl, which resulted in the untimely death of a teenager from Baschurch. She was killed crossing the line behind the train from which she had descended, on the Wrexham side, by a goods train which was not required to stop at Baschurch.

Nowadays not much happens at the station. Passenger trains no longer stop, and Myddle gets all its supplies by road.

As I have said, the horse provided almost all the transport that was ever needed in those days. Until the time of my departure from Myddle, farmers relied solely on the horse for all agricultural tasks. A two- or three-horse team and usually two men were employed in ploughing. A harsh farmer would insist on his men working in all weathers, however difficult the task. Old sacks would then be wrapped around shoulders and legs in an attempt to prevent wet seeping to the next layer of clothing for as long as possible.

My sister Dorothy, however, remembers the time when radical changes began to occur, which were eventually to render the horse redundant. She recalls the mighty rumbling sound, like distant thunder, which caused small children to run out of their cottages, teachers to pause momentarily in their lessons, and women to stop their conversations. It was the arrival of a giant steam traction-engine, thundering its way along the unsurfaced road; smoke, exhaust steam and sparks emitting from the tall funnel. The huge iron wheels turned slowly, and one was conscious of the distinctive beat of the massive vehicle. There was usually a box in tow, which was a thrashing machine. The route past our cottage was invariably taken by this monster, to avoid the steep bank; but once round the corner past the quarry, more coal would be shovelled into the firebox to aid the steady climb up Myddle Hill. Thick black smoke belched out, coupled with the smell of oil. These machines incorporated an enormous coal box and water tank, and sometimes a canopy covered the engine. Their presence in the village was not uncommon at harvest time, when farmers hired the engines for a few days.

Unfortunately, this new visitor presented another hazard for Marjorie's mother (of whom more later) who, fearful of a spark on her thatch, would appear at the gate in her little cotton bonnet. Buckets of water were hastily drawn from the brook adjacent to her garden and, with an old pump, she sprayed water on the thatch closest to the lane. There was a very real possibility that a spark from a traction engine might cause a fire, especially in a period of dry weather.

It was traction engines and other new-fangled machinery which were eventually to sound the death-knell of the village farrier.

The old forge at the top of Myddle Bank presents a sorry sight nowadays. As more motor vehicles came on to the roads and more machinery was used in the fields, the ancient skills of the blacksmith were less needed as time went by. However, in other towns and villages the blacksmith gradually turned his attention to the complex tasks involved in keeping the early motor cars, lorries and steam-wagons on the road, and in the early days of motoring, the hammer and the anvil were sometimes just as useful as the more complicated equipment used today. Thus the village blacksmith would gradually evolve into the modern service station, often continuing to use the same buildings.

This did not happen at Myddle. The last working blacksmith and farrier was Mr Neale of Webscott. A fascinating variety of work went on at the forge in the 1920s.

The forge lay at the junction of Myddle Hill and Myddle Bank at a point where it could easily be seen by traffic on the top highway, and where a smithy had stood for generations. The single-storey sandstone workshop nestled comfortably at the roadside. It was the first impression one gained of the village upon entering, and the final memory on departure. When village lads left to go to the Great War, many never to return, the forge would be their last sight of Myddle on the walk to Yorton Station.

The lower section of the workshop accommodated Mr Hodnet's wheelwright shop, where he made and repaired wheels, posts, gates, carts, etc. He lived at the sandstone cottage opposite, with its neat iron railings fabricated at the forge.

There was usually an untidy assortment of farm implements awaiting repair or collection, littering the waste ground between the cottage and the smithy.

Before the era of the internal combustion engine, both the blacksmith and the wheelwright were without doubt the most important tradesmen in the village, to whom everyone turned at one time or another. Apart from the obvious shoeing of horses and repairs to farm implements, Mr Neale found time to keep children happy with Victorian Bowlers, popular playthings of the day, consisting of a wheel and handle, which he made for 2d each. Mr Neale obliged Father by forging an iron balustrade to define the boundary of the front raised walk between the cottages. Being the excellent craftsman that he was, the ironwork was functional and sturdy, whilst at the same time ornamental.

The open doorway of the forge was a favourite gathering-place for children, where tiny boys dreamed of becoming

Mr Neale the blacksmith, in the doorway of Myddle Forge.
In Helen's youth this was always a focal point of village life – with a
miscellaneous assortment of farm implements awaiting repair, as
seen here.

apprentices to Mr Neale upon attaining their 14th birthday. The
familiar figure of Mr Neale in cap and long leather apron, which
protected him to some degree from the intense heat and sparks
from the furnace, was distinguishable on a winter evening in the
orange glow, back bent, hammer banging, sparks flying. Making
shoes was certainly no simple matter, as we learned, watching
them returned to the forge many times for shaping.

My sister Dorothy, the youngest in our family, recalls that
as quite small children, Mr Neale allowed them to gather in the
smithy while he put shoes on the big shire horses (the gentle
giants – they were lovely). He also let them have a go on the
bellows and make the sparks fly. He was a lovely, kindly man.

Mr Neale lived to the age of 88 at Brook Cottage, Webscott,
which is described in another chapter. His predecessor had

Myddle smithy, always
surrounded by an assortment
of carts and wheels in need of repair.

been Mr Hales, who lived close to the forge. Modern museums
sometimes house collections of wagons, ploughs and other farm
implements from this and earlier periods. Looking at these
collections, it is amazing to realise that even as late as the 1920s,
complete wagons, drays and carts, in fact anything which a
horse would pull on the lanes or in the fields, would be made at
a village forge, relying entirely on the skills of the blacksmith,
wheelwright and carpenter, all living in or near the village
and using skills and methods which were handed down from
generation to generation. Sadly, by the time of my childhood,
manufacture of these goods was becoming less common in
villages; blacksmiths and wheelwrights (unless they branched
out into the new-fangled motor trade) tended to concentrate on
repairing the old wagons and farm implements, which would
provide much less work in the years to come.

The redundant building standing at the top of Myddle
Bank today is regarded with affection by older residents, its rich
brown-red-cream sandstone blocks ageing gracefully. It bears
its own silent testimony to the decay of the village forge in the
age of the motor car and the mass-produced artifacts of today.
The lower double doors of the wheelwright's shop are still a
target for fly-posters advertising local events, as they were over
50 years ago.

Tree felling was another local trade. When I was young the tree fellers would move from one area to another as necessary, but I can remember the time when Father received news (which spreads at an incredible speed in a small village) that Myddle coppice was to be felled. The coppice was situated between Mrs Watkins' pretty sandstone cottage at the top of Lower Road, and the cottages immediately under the hill at Webscott.

The opportunity to acquire a free source of firewood was not to be missed, and Father gave us instructions accordingly. After school each afternoon we were to proceed to the coppice with truck and sacks, our pockets bulging with bits of binder twine. We watched the sturdy timber-fellers who took up positions at each side of the tree with sharp long axes. They chipped off flat pieces of wood which whistled through the air, as blades cut deeper into the trunk. After the tree had fallen, we ran forward together, filling our sacks with the chippings. The men had been working all day and we soon found enough wood to fill them. All this was to save a few pence on coal.

Strong chains were attached to the felled trees, which were then dragged to the lane by two large horses. A great deal of skill was required to load the trunks onto a flat wagon; but eventually this complex procedure was complete, and the wagon was drawn to the siding at Yorton Station from where the timber was transported.

At the end of the day, after very hard work, the horses were led to a nearby field. As soon as the gate was opened and the horses let loose inside, they would run and gallop round the field, then roll on their backs (but not completely over). After this ritual, they got back on their feet and began to graze. Early next morning, long before the men arrived, the horses would be waiting at the gate, ready for another hard day's work! They were magnificent large brown wagon horses, with white faces, hooves dyed orange from the sand in which they worked.

These chippings, together with the small amount of coal we purchased, kept us warm in the cottage for many months, and produced a most pleasing odour when burning. After clearance of the woodland, a public footpath was opened to link with the Higher Road, near aunt Ethel Hushand's cottage, this being specially useful in the winter and acting as a short-cut to the church and to the village.

Another village trader, who lived among the working villagers at Myddlewood, was Mr Brookfield the saddler. I have made no mention of him previously, as our way of life was not one which ever called upon the services of a saddler. But he was important in the age of the horse. His father had lived and worked at the same premises before him – a cottage and workshop with a half-closing stable-type door, on the Fenemere Road next to the Reading Room, and taught his son the trade. Here he made and repaired saddles, harnesses, bridles, boots, collars and leggings.

Like me, these trades have all left Myddle. Nowadays horses are shod (those few horses which remain) by a man who visits farms as required, carrying his equipment in a Land Rover. Saddles and harnesses have to be bought in nearby towns. These trades are no longer carried on in Myddle and the village is the poorer for it.

The Old Smithy, Myddle, drawn by Elizabeth Brown

CHAPTER TWENTY

The Village Postmistress/Seamstress

The village Postmistress was Mrs Yeomans, and her cottage from where business was conducted, was just beyond our terrace. It was built on a flat rock outcrop above the lane, approached by a small flight of well-worn stone steps. This construction was yet another example of early building skills.

Our cottage was built on the same outcrop – Father grumbled that he couldn't dig far down in our garden before encountering rock. Thus serious vegetable growing was undertaken in our top field.

To return to the Post Office, a half-closing door, with shelf, served as a counter, with a bell to ring for attention. We never entered the cottage. In those days the Post Office was not unduly busy and Mrs Yeomans found time to act as village seamstress.

She eventually married a widower, Mr Bourne, who had experience of shopkeeping, and they moved into the village store when this became vacant. This accommodation was roomy with six bedrooms and ample space for shop, granary and Post Office. A section of the heavy wooden counter, nearest the living room, was set aside for Post Office business, so that Mrs Bourne could easily be called for when required.

In a corner of their garden, opposite our cottage, stood an ancient dark-leaved yew tree, the healthy scent of which filled our bedroom after a shower of rain. Mother purchased all our provisions from their store.

I saw my first bride when I was about six years old. Mother

took me along and we stood by the wall outside the lych gate. The then-Rector, Reverend Edgerton, brought his daughter to be married. She wore a long white dress made by the village Post Mistress, a lace veil, and carried flowers. Thereafter my greatest delight was to observe weddings.

Women tended to wear hats in those days, indeed Mother rarely ventured out of doors without hers. Hats were simple, sensible felt cloche or straw affairs, mostly second-hand, usually battered and faded and certainly well loved. Farmers' wives liked to keep up appearances, especially when attending church services. They possessed an air of ruddy charm and rural elegance, and quite often purchased a new hat when shopping in town, although not a complete outfit. Thus it was that their redundant millinery became available to village women through jumble sales, hat stalls at fêtes and so on.

Generally, a small length of petersham ribbon, purchased at the cottage door from a pedlar or gipsy, transformed the hats beyond immediate recognition.

Mr and Mrs Bourne were regular worshippers at the Primitive Methodist Chapel at Webscott, where Mr Bourne often preached. They walked along the Lower Road on Sunday evenings or took the field path in the summer.

Mrs Bourne was the designer of some very stylish outfits which she made for farmers' wives. One particular lavender outfit she made and wore herself was quite special, as we lived in a navy, brown and black world! It was designed in lavender wool, comprising a long flared skirt, matching tightly-fitted jacket with large pleated sleeves. A lavender straw hat which she had trimmed with tulle and flowers complemented the outfit.

It was lovely!

CHAPTER TWENTY ONE

Younger Sister Dorothy

When my youngest sister Dorothy attained the age of 14, my parents decided that instead of working on a farm she should apply for a position at the Rectory, where there was a vacancy for a maid. She would then be close at hand if Mother was ill.

The Rectory, a rambling 18th century red brick house, largely concealed beneath an abundance of creeper, was situated opposite the church. The house was of immense proportions with later Victorian extensions at the side. The main staircase was of white stone, and very imposing, sweeping around into the vast hall. No carpets were permitted to envelop its magnificent surface. It was, of course, only used by family; the maids used another staircase on the kitchen side of the house.

For most of Dorothy's stay she was the only permanent member of staff. Another maid came, and went, leaving on the pretext that her attic bedroom was haunted. She was not replaced. With the exception of cooking, which was undertaken by the rector's wife, and heavy work tackled by a robust village woman who came in on certain days, Dorothy coped with all other household chores herself in this vast ecclesiastical residence. The Rectory was lit by oil lamps, placed on polished oak tables in the lounge, dining room and study, with candles for bedtime use.

On the whole my sister was very happy working here – until the Rector's daughter came to live with her parents, bringing her new baby; her husband was in the services. She accompanied her parents frequently on parish visits, and it was Dorothy's task to look after the baby during their absence.

My sister was very fond of the Rector and his daughter, who were both kind to her, but she rather hated this new aspect of her duties. She knew little about infants, being the youngest of a large family. She asked our parents if she might seek employment elsewhere, but they quickly dismissed the suggestion as quite unthinkable, saying she couldn't possibly let the Rector down. So she continued until the position became quite intolerable and she felt she could endure life at the Rectory no longer.

She carefully devised a plan to be implemented at the earliest opportunity. Later that week, when she calculated everyone was asleep, she lit the candle and reached down her case from the wardrobe top. She began to pack. This took some time as drawers had to be opened and closed silently. Eventually this task was complete and the lid closed and secured. Her bedroom was devoid of a clock, so she made her way surreptitiously down the back stairs to consult the clock on the kitchen wall.

She had no desire to take down the case until after 5am and so she sat on her bed and waited, watching the melted wax drip down the candle and hoping that the diminishing light would last until her departure. When she calculated that sufficient time had elapsed, candle in one hand, weighty case in the other, she crept stealthily down the maid's staircase and into the kitchen. Her case was impossibly heavy and she could carry it for only a few yards at a time; thus the passage from the kitchen to the tradesmen's entrance seemed endless. She had no difficulty turning the large key in the door – she was out! Down the drive she tiptoed, resting for a few brief moments with the case. Next she opened the large gate, the hinges squeaking loudly for want of oil. She held her breath – all was still silent. She stopped every few yards with the case which became heavier with each step. It was no good, she could carry the burden no longer, so she hid it in the bushes near the school.

Now for it, she thought, collywobbles rumbling, she went up to our cottage door and knocked hard. Father appeared at the bedroom window and upon seeing his daughter, disappeared

Youngest sister Dorothy ran away from her Rectory job at 5am one morning. She is pictured here, in happier times, on the roadway outside.

downstairs and let her in. He was too dazed and startled to take it all in at first, but agreed to throw an old coat over his shoulders and retrieve the case. Mother was dumbfounded – never in our family had anything like this happened, and running away from the Rectory, of all places! They were all for taking her back there and then, before her absence was discovered. But Dorothy stamped her feet on the floor, declaring if she went back, she would run away again! Eventually she wore them down, and they agreed that she should not go back. The kindly Rector completely forgave Dorothy for what she had done, and they remained good friends. He even brought round a pair of wellingtons which she had omitted to pack!

DOROTHY'S NEXT JOB

She quickly found another position at Old Hall, Merrington in the service of Miss Sybil Kenyon Slaney. This distinguished lady spent many weeks with Princess Mary at Harewood House near Harrogate or at the Duchess of Kent's home 'Coppins', Iver, Buckinghamshire, as Lady-in-Waiting.

Old Hall was a charming farmhouse, with an abundance of oak beams and oak floors which sloped at different angles; furniture had to be supported by blocks to keep it straight. It was a fairly small house with four bedrooms in all. Miss Kenyon Slaney kept six sheep which were really pets to keep the grass short in the orchard.

Near the house was a lovely old-fashioned garden with several shady arbors to which one could retreat. Dorothy accompanied the chauffeur on sheep-dip excursions across Merrington Green to a farm known as 'Williams the Hayes'.

Bees were also kept in the orchard, and in spare moments Dorothy helped by making the sections which held the honey. When full these were sold for one shilling.

When Dorothy left Old Hall to enlist, Miss Kenyon Slaney gave her a tiny pair of scissors and a penknife on a cord, as a keepsake. Dot carried them with her all through her WAAF years.

CHAPTER 22

How World War II Affected Us All

By the start of World War II, I had long-since vacated Myddle, acquired a husband, home, daughter, and my son was born during an air raid in 1940 over Birmingham.

Meanwhile, back in Myddle, three of my siblings were enlisting. Mother was to have three of her children in the forces.

Brother Harry

Posted to 58/69 Field Coy RE India Command
Harry was one of many injured and sent home from Burma.

Brother Jack

Desperately wanted to join the RAF but he was working on a Chicken Farm and was told that this was a Reserved Occupation, feeding the nation. Eventually, however, he was given permission to join and came out class B at the end of hostilities.

Sister Dorothy

Trained as a Flight Mechanic at RAF Cranwell (Lincolnshire). She became a Leading Aircraftswoman and remained with Training Command – 17 Service Training School. The work was very dirty: they were called 'grease monkeys' and had to sign for every job completed on an aircraft.

"With Love from Harry"
Christmas 1944.
But before the war ended, Harry
was shot through the leg and
invalided home.

She found it especially rewarding to watch pilots getting their wings. Often the WAAFS would stitch these on for new pilots, so that they could go out the same day and show them off to their friends!

During a period of leave at Myddle she purchased a newspaper at Shrewsbury Station and on the front page was news of the Flight Commander of one of their flights, whom she knew quite well. He had been posted onto Hawker 'Typhoons' fighter/ bombers, and had been in action over France when his aircraft had sustained severe damage and he had made a spectacular flight back to England with three feet of one wing missing. He was an amazing man, admired by everyone in the unit, and always wore a distinctive black leather flying suit.

At the end of hostilities, when members of the forces returned to Myddle, they were each given a cash sum and an illuminated address, with name, service and the flags of the three services shown at the top.

Dorothy's read:

The Parish of Myddle in the County of Shropshire honours her sons and daughters who, during the years 1939-1945 took up arms in defence of their country, on land, on sea, and in the air. At home and abroad they willingly embraced every danger and discomfort, that we might remain free. She salutes on her return
DOROTHY EBREY
of whose loyal service and self-sacrifice she will ever be mindful.

Signed
John Parker, Chairman of Committee, Balderton Hall
John Griffiths, Honorary Secretary, Houlston Manor Farm

All members of the forces returning to Myddle after the war received an illuminated address – this is merely a copy of my sister Dot's.

Dorothy later married her RAF Sergeant in Myddle Church and was then spirited away to his home county of Kent, where they lived happily together until the end of their lives.

Later Dorothy joined the WAAF, becoming a 'grease monkey', the RAF's unflattering term for a female Flight Mechanic. She is seen here in her RAF uniform at RAF Cranwell (Lincs) in 1944, aged 20

OTHER WARTIME OCCUPATIONS

There were other wartime-related occupations which Myddle girls undertook. Three of these are detailed below:

LUMBER JILL

Friend Joan, who later married my brother Jack, had a difficult job working at a timber yard at Wem (Isherwoods). This had previously been regarded as a man's job – but all the men had gone to war. [Years later Joan was presented with a Badge of Honour for Lumber Jills by Hilary Benn – Secretary of State for Environment Food and Rural Affairs.]

SIGNALWOMAN

Sister Elsie became a Signalwoman working for London Midland and Scottish Railway at Yorton Station. She had to pass a test and medical at Crewe, which she did, and spent part of the war in the wooden signal box at Yorton Station. She manipulated heavy levers which operated points and signals, because all the men had gone to war.

LAND ARMY

Friend Annie joined the Land Army, the group of women organised during the war for farm work. Farms were charged with feeding the nation during World War II.

OPERATION STARFISH

Whixall Moss, a large expanse of peat, nine miles north of Myddle (from which Granny Ebrey had purchased peat for burning from an old woman with horse and cart who called at Myddle) was given an interesting role during World War II.

It was used as a decoy by the MoD in an endeavour to trick German bombers into thinking the Moss was Liverpool – some 35 miles away. When word reached that bombers were on their way, fire baskets (60 or so) were lit over the moss to resemble street patterns.

BOMBER CRASH

In 1942 a Whitley Bomber crashed in Myddle village after taking off from nearby Sleap Airfield.

CHAPTER 23

My First Job

I left Myddle School in 1925 at the age of 14.

My parents arranged for Emily (my 16-year-old sister) and me, to commence work at a farm some distance from the village centre. Em had not hitherto worked, being a delicate child prone to heavy nosebleeds. The positions were described as 'general workers', which basically covered all aspects of farm work and the long, long hours – 6am usually until 9pm, minus short half-hour breaks for breakfast, dinner and supper. There were no coffee/tea breaks in those days and we worked a 7-day week.

It was customary to live-in and we were given a small cold bedroom to share. We saw our parents on Sunday evenings, after milking, when we attended the Parish Church together and took our dirty clothes home for Mother to wash, this being the agreement with the farm. We had nothing to eat after dinner at the farm on Sundays until breakfast after milking next morning. Mother said now that we were working she had no responsibility to feed us!

Our shortage of food generally and the absence of meat in our diet at home resulted in us both being slight in build, and not strong enough for this type of heavy work.

Emily had never seen a doctor about the recurring nosebleeds; Mother simply laid her on the cold kitchen floor and placed our enormous door-key down her back, which usually did the trick.

Every penny we earned had to be handed over to Mother. We each earned 5/- (five shillings) per week. It went into her tea-caddy towards payments for the cottage.

To return to farm-work, we were called at 6am to hand-milk 16 cows before breakfast. We sat on little 3-legged milking stools. Em was often pushed by a cow, which triggered a heavy nosebleed; she was instructed by the master to continue milking – her blood trickling into the cowshed drain.

A cowman helped me load the heavy churns of milk onto a wagon (except when we turned milk into cheese), but I had to lead the horse down the track to the lane and get the churns off the wagon myself and onto the stand, without assistance. Here they awaited collection by the local carrier, Mr Hignett, to Baschurch Station, where the yard would be congested by wagon-loads of milk-churns coming from all directions.

However, when we made cheese most of the milk was poured directly into large vats and we retained just sufficient milk for everyday domestic use.

To return to the farm. Thursday nights were worst of all, for it was on Thursdays that the master took the pony and trap to Wem market to sell eggs. Emily and I had previously washed the eggs carefully and placed them with straw into large market baskets. After leaving the horse with the ostler at the inn for a few hours, the master negotiated the sale of the consignment of eggs to a market trader. He then returned to the inn where he met up with other farmers he knew, and enjoyed a meal with them, accompanied by plenty of ale.

The drinking continued all afternoon. How he got home I never knew, for he couldn't stand. Fortunately the horse knew the way back and brought master and trap into the yard. Somehow we all struggled to get him out of the trap and into the house, whereupon a dreadful quarrel would ensue with his poor wife, for he was a man who could not take drink.

These noisy hostilities continued long after our bedtime, and into the small hours of the morning, culminating with the (by now) extremely violent farmer procuring his shotgun from between leather straps fixed to the oak beams of the parlour ceiling. Emily and I wondered whether he was really more mad than drunk, because getting the gun out of straps in the ceiling was actually quite a complicated operation.

At this dangerous stage our distressed mistress, fearful of her life, converged upon Emily and I, together with her sobbing children. They didn't wake us from our sleep, for we had none during these regular nights of terror.

Why she should seek our little bedroom as a safe haven from him we could not understand, for it was only fitted with a latch door: there was no means of barricading ourselves in until morning when the men arrived for work. She seemed to think he wouldn't dare follow her into our room, but by so doing she put Emily and I, her paid workers, into the firing line. He was so close, just the other side of an unlocked door. Here he positioned himself for what seemed like hours, banging the loaded shotgun against the door, shouting violent abuse, and threatening to kill us all!

My sister and I lay huddled in our bed, the bedclothes pulled over our heads to try and stifle the horror and threats of death. We prayed, as we had been taught at Sunday School to pray. But he continued and we became more and more terrified, and the mistress just sobbed and tried to comfort her own children. She sat shaking at the foot of our bed clutching them, for there was no chair in the room, which was in darkness, candles having long been extinguished. He continued storming about outside in the passage, like a madman, banging the butt of the gun against the walls, and swearing that we should soon all die. We really thought our last moments had come, and had no hope of ever seeing the light of dawn or our parents again.

Eventually, however, the consequences of tiredness and violence overcame the master and he either crumpled onto the wooden floor, or stumbled back to his room. When this happened and the mistress felt it was safe to creep back with the children, she left us. But we had suffered an immense shock and were much too frightened to sleep; we lay awake listening to every sound and creak the old farmhouse made, until 6am when we were called for milking as usual.

Later that morning, the master would take us aside and we would again be threatened, but this time never to divulge to anyone the previous night's happenings.

Of course we did. We both pleaded with our parents to be permitted to be released from the atrocious happenings, which occurred on a 7-day cycle. We told them our lives were in danger. But they were quite indifferent to our plight, and it was almost as though they thought Emily and I had fabricated the story to facilitate our departure. In those days children, especially poor children, had no voice whatsoever. And so, after Sunday evening worship, we were accompanied back to the farm by Mother, week after miserable week, for two years. The repeated discourse and pleadings with our parents were to no avail.

I should explain that Sundays at the farmhouse were a little different from the usual run-of-the-mill oppression. On the Sabbath a more convivial atmosphere exuded into the old rooms, the mistress lighting a fire in the front sitting room, where they had their tea. But we had to leave to be in time for church, so a place at the table was never set for Em and I. After their tea, a Victorian-style musical evening took place, with the family sitting around the comfortable room singing hymns.

The master, who had a good singing voice, accompanied them on the organ. So happy were these occasions that the family were often still singing at 9pm, when we returned, and the music was just discernible from the lane on warm summer evenings. Mother, fearful that we might be molested, walked back to the farm with us. She quite wrongly assumed from the hymn-singing that life here was happy and that we worked in amicable surroundings. She could not have been more mistaken.

Returning to our farm duties: I helped when ploughing. My job was to lead the first of two horses. This I did for the whole morning and again after lunch. The ground was uneven and I disliked the job; the horse was immense and towered above me – for I was not very tall. It was a single plough and only one row could be completed at a time. Mother was required to provide our clogs to wear, and these we had to scrub before entering the farmhouse. They were necessarily strong and fastened tightly with buckles on the side. Mother's hand-knitted socks came just over the knee.

If the weather was too rough for field work, the men were found work in the barns and cow-sheds, white-washing, or repairing woodwork and mangers, or cleaning the master's trap under cover.

When we turned our attention to cheese-making, a buyer came from Wem to test our product. Using a long bore, which he stuck into the cheese, he was able to cut a piece from the centre for tasting. If he found the cheese satisfactory, he would purchase all that we had produced. Emily and I carried the cheeses from an upper room where they had been put to dry. We then pasted them with thin cotton cheese cloth; first over each end, pulled very tightly, and then over the centre. This helped to preserve the cheese and keep it firm. We then loaded them onto the dray, between generous cushions of straw to prevent bruising in transit. The farmer drove the consignment to the shop in Wem from where it was sold to the public.

No doubt it was more profitable to produce cheese than sell milk, for we certainly made substantial quantities. The pigs benefitted when we made cheese from the unwanted sweet whey, drawn off the milk, which was fed to them!

Having spent the whole day engaged on gruelling farm work, we were forced to be domestic servants for the remainder of the evening. Emily and I were required to wash the children and put them to bed, then wash up the dinner dishes. After this, the children's clothes had to be washed and hung out in the yard.

When very young, the children attended a private school in the village, located in Mrs Flannigan's front parlour. The school was popular with farmers' children who were too young for the village school, tuition being provided by a teacher. We helped prepare the children for school, dressing them, brushing their hair, lacing up boots, etc – this was after the morning milking, and before our long day's work.

On dark winter evenings when the farmer ran out of logs for the fire, Em and I were despatched with a hurricane-lamp to the barn, where we were instructed to put logs on a trestle and saw them between us. We placed the cut logs into sacks, which were exceptionally heavy, then carried or dragged the sacks back to the farmhouse as best we could. This was undeniably man's work.

During our period of servitude, the master foolishly packed hay too tightly in the barn, not allowing sufficient ventilation. The resultant barn fire was the worst the neighbourhood had known. We were aroused from our sleep to help fight the fire. Emily and I were justifiably frightened when we saw the barn; the hay was well alight with flames leaping high into the night sky. The farmer handed us buckets to fill with water from the well in the yard, and shouted his instruction that we throw water into the fire in a futile effort to suppress the flames.

The solitary owner of a telephone at that time was Mr Bourne at Myddle Post Office, so the master legged it to the village to wake him. This kindly man was only too pleased to help, despite the hour, and rang for the fire brigade in Wem. Meanwhile at the farm, we were astonished at the arrival of our neighbours who had come to offer assistance. They gladly volunteered to carry water to the fire. Eventually, the horse-drawn fire contraption arrived from Wem. The men lost no time in getting hoses fixed upon the blaze, and we then became spectators for a short time, as they took over. The fire was finally brought under control at around 6am.

The mistress invited the firemen into the kitchen and cooked them a ham and egg breakfast. Before leaving, however, the head fireman gave a word of caution to the master, on methods of packing hay into a barn.

Meanwhile, an exhausted Emily and I were despatched – not to bed – but to milk the cows as usual. We later helped spread the burnt hay over the fields.

We were never given sufficient to eat; our diet was quite inadequate for the heavy nature of our duties. We survived largely by cutting a wedge of cheese for ourselves whenever sent to the cheese-room. If the farmer had discovered our secret, the consequences could have been dire

A deep well was situated in the yard, near the back door from which we drew water for cooling the vats in cheese-making and for washing milking vessels, and so on (there were always a hundred jobs for us to do). This supply was not suitable for drinking; drinking water was piped to the farmhouse from a well in one of the fields. It entered the house via the cellar, and we had to go down a short flight of steps to collect it. During the summer months, the water level dropped, so we had to take buckets and a piece of rope, lift the grid off the well, drop the bucket down the shaft by rope, and carry the precious drinking water back along the field.

Milking pails were kept clean with boiling water: no soap or soda were ever used. They were turned upside down and placed on a little stand, with no cover, out in the cobbled yard. Being exposed to the elements, when we came to use them they were often cold, wet and slippery, or sometimes covered with snow. And in this state, of course, were placed between our knees. The warm milk from the cow did eventually warm the bucket, and us!

Another of our many duties was to swill and brush down the cobbled yards every week, to prevent slippery moss getting a hold on the stones.

Washing ourselves was a real problem. We didn't have a bath in two years (how we must have smelled!) nor were we allowed to take a bowl of water upstairs to the privacy of our room. Everyone had to wash in the kitchen. Our shoulder-length hair was another problem which we overcame by going out of doors during a heavy shower and getting it soaked. We then rubbed it dry on a towel and this is how we managed for 24 months. When people were frail, like my sister, these were the circumstances which could so easily have brought on pneumonia. (Our employers performed their own ablutions while Em and I were at church on Sunday evenings.)

Eventually, after almost two years of this arduous life and the repeated threats to our lives, circumstances began to change in our favour. Firstly, there was the David Lloyd George Act, requiring employers to contribute towards pensions for employees, which the farmer was not keen on doing. Secondly, we were aided by local gossip!

Somehow news began to filter through to the village of the sinister 'carryings on' at the lonely farmhouse when the farmer became drunk. We never knew the origins of the rumours, but Emily and I were eternally grateful to the perpetrators.

We could only speculate that it might have been someone poaching near the farmhouse on a Thursday evening, because being so far from the lane, there was no chance of a passer-by hearing the furore. Anyway our prayers had been answered; when local people, whom Father respected, told him they would not allow *their* daughters to work at the farm, the seed of doubt was eventually sown in his mind. We were told we might leave. The mistress, however, didn't want us to go; she offered an inducement of a small increase in pay and a few days unpaid holiday, if we would stay. But nothing could possibly have persuaded us to continue this miserable life for a day longer than necessary.

I valued my sister's company enormously during these two years. However bad things were, we endured everything together.

The farmer did eventually pull the trigger – but not until much later when Emily and I were miles from Myddle. I cannot give details, for family members may still remain in the area.

The farmer desperately needed help, but there was none available in those days.

*****

I had not wanted this farm job at all. My first ambition upon leaving school was to become a scullery maid, which was the sort of job that girls like myself from farm-labourers' families usually took when we left school at 14.

There had been a vacancy at Shotton Hall, for which Mother arranged for me to apply. When I arrived, the housekeeper took me into the resplendent oak-panelled drawing-room to meet the Marchioness of Cambridge, who was sitting by the fireside, her dogs at her feet.

I curtsied. I thought the room in which I stood exceedingly beautiful; the pale blue carpet and blue brocade cushions and curtains with silk tassels were delightful to the eye. It immediately occurred to me how pleasing it would be to live and work in such admirable surroundings, and my heart raced with excitement. However, it was not to be, for the Marchioness eyed me shrewdly and said, kindly, that she didn't think I was strong enough to lift the large iron pans off the range and into the sink.

I am sure she was right. We never really had enough food at home. She was very sorry, but would I tell Mother that in her opinion, I should be seeking lighter work!

MOVING ON

Girls like me applying for domestic posts were, of course, completely at the mercy of prospective employers. In those days so many girls wanted to be maids, with the result that an employer could afford to turn a girl down for really trivial reasons. An example of this occurred when I applied for a position at Shrewsbury School as a maid. The housekeeper interviewed me, but she seemed rather pre-occupied during our talk by the fact that I now wore spectacles, enquiring if they were absolutely necessary and whether I could manage without them. She concluded by saying that if they were essential, then the school might be able to consider me for the vacancy.

Many girls were interviewed that day, and I didn't hear any more. I assumed the position had been offered to a non-spectacled applicant! She did however reimburse my travelling expenses, and the nominal charge that I had incurred in crossing the River Severn by the toll bridge from the town to the school.

*****

Emily obtained a live-in post with the Parkers of Balderton Hall, the magnificent farmhouse where Father had been employed when I was born and where he remained until enlisting in 1914. The family were very kind to Mother while Emily worked there, as indeed they had been to Father. Emily loved working there immensely.

*****

When sister Elsie's turn came to leave school at 14 (she was four years younger than me) she was sent by our parents to do general work at Castle Farm, where she was very happy. Although so close to home, she had to live at the farm, as was the system.

CHAPTER 24

Mr Hamilton the Vet at Baschurch

After my disastrous job at the farm, I was successful in applying for a position as a general maid in the home of Mr Hamilton, an erudite Scottish gentleman, at Baschurch some three miles from Myddle. He was the only Vet in the area.

The family were extremely kind to me and I tried to put aside the terrifying memories of the past two years. My room was in the attic, quite a pleasant little room with views across the village.

I rose early and cleaned the Victorian house before breakfast. There were two young children in the family and I often accompanied the small boy to the nearby station, if his mother was indisposed. He caught a daily train to school in Shrewsbury.

The station I found interesting, it possessed a fine group of buildings and was somewhat larger and more impressive than my recollections of Yorton.

When folk called at the house to collect drugs for their animals, I handed the labelled package to them. This aspect of my new position I rather enjoyed as it was pleasant to meet members of the community after the isolation of the farm. In those days farmers did not possess telephones. Someone would call personally either by bike, or by horseback when the vet was required and leave directions to their farm. Drugs were dispensed from Mr Hamilton's small office, but if he should be called away in an emergency, he brought the package into the

A round six-mile walk took Helen back home every Sunday afternoon to the familiar sight of her village of Myddle, as seen from the quarry lane.

Myddle, Shropshire.

kitchen, telling us who would be coming. Being the only vet in the area and because of the distances he travelled, he possessed a little car.

Annually, in August, he engaged a temporary vet who travelled down from Scotland, so that Mr Hamilton and the family could take a holiday.

My Sunday afternoons were free almost every week, and I walked home and back (six miles). I was still working a very long six-day week, with duties on both Sunday mornings and Sunday evenings in addition, but this would have been regarded as quite normal at the time; it would not have occurred to people in domestic service to worry about excessively long hours, however low the wages were.

My earnings were, in fact, 7/6d weekly, all of which Mother took from me – but this seemed a princely sum after the five shillings which I had earned at the farm, doing heavier work and existing in fear of my life for much of the time.

Mrs Hamilton came from the north of Scotland. She cooked lovely meals and had numerous ways of cooking fish which she taught me. Fish was a dish I had never tasted – we didn't have it at home!

I was exceptionally happy working here, but determined that if a position should arise in the future to take me away from the area, I would apply.

To avoid eviction of the family, Helen's father *(back row, right)* managed to buy the family cottage from the Estate, but repaying the loan had a major effect on Helen's (and her siblings') childhood. Here, many years later in 1947, he is seen outside Myddle Church at Helen's sister Dorothy's wedding to ex-RAF flight sergeant Sid Collison from Kent. Helen's mother stands in front, while sister Elsie does the honours as bridesmaid. Elizabeth, who transcribed this account from interviews with her mother, but who was then an excited 8-year-old with younger brother in tow, recalls that afterwards guests were taken by hired coach to a café in Wem for the reception.

CHAPTER 25

Leaving

I was working at Baschurch when I responded to an advertisement in the *Wellington Journal* for the position of a house/parlour maid at Birkenhead.

The mistress came by rail to interview me and this she did in Mother's parlour. I seemed to answer all her questions correctly and I was accepted. Soon after, I departed for the home of cotton merchants in Birkenhead. I knew little about the town but discovered that it was about sixty miles from Myddle by a circuitous route. Also, it was on the River Mersey, with a ferry across to Liverpool, and ships were built there.

Mother had helped me carry a large black painted wooden box the three miles from Myddle to Baschurch station. It contained my bare necessities. Mother had made me a petticoat with wide shoulder-straps, which would double as a nightdress, so she said. She also made two pairs of knickers (which were all I had); two aprons and caps. My regulation black stockings had to be purchased. She had sewn a black cotton frock, and I recall how cold the large house was, and how inadequate this thin dress. Mother was still taking all our money – I had no cash to buy warmer clothes.

I had strict instructions to post all my earnings to her until I was 21. (This instruction applied to all my siblings. She called at the farms to collect the boys' wages. My sisters usually went home on Sunday evenings.)

For the journey to Birkenhead I wore an old suit which Aunt Lizzie from Crewe had kindly given me.

I did not possess a winter coat but a cook from a nearby residence, whom I befriended by walking to church along the same route, sold me her old coat for four shillings when she bought a new one. On this occasion I defied Mother and retained the cost of the old coat.

I was not at all happy working here. One evening I was reprimanded by the mistress for leaving the house without a hat, to post a letter home!

I moved to Birkenhead completely against my parents' wishes, and was the first in my family to move so far away from home for employment. I had resolutely decided to take the step to achieve a degree of independence.

I was now constantly searching for a more amicable position. I had no wish to return to Shropshire and no wish to remain here!

Helen at her wedding to Harold Ivings,
Handsworth (Birmingham) in 1937

POSTSCRIPT

My mother Helen had left Myddle in 1928 aged 17, for domestic service in Birkenhead. This was one of the few openings available to a village girl at the time. She soon moved to Handsworth in Birmingham, still in domestic service. But at last she had found a kindly mistress – who went so far as to provide a wedding breakfast when she eventually married in 1937.

In later life Helen told me the story of her childhood years, in the hope that this would be of interest to future generations.

She never had any regrets about leaving Myddle. Even after sixty years of town and city life, mostly in a small terraced house in Hamstead (an edge-of-Birmingham colliery village), she had no illusions about village life in the early years of the last century.

'Tall trees and green fields never provided me with a living,' she used to say.

Helen and her husband Harold both died in 1997. Helen was 86 years old.

Elizabeth Brown (Helen's daughter) 2016

Helen aged 61 with daughter Elizabeth on the occasion of a grandson's christening in Harrogate, Yorkshire. Helen had made both coats. Her sewing classes at the old Myddle Vicarage, some 50 years previously, had clearly not been in vain.

Also by Merlin Unwin Books

Wild Flower's of Britain *Month by Month*
   Margaret Erskine Wilson

A Shropshire Lad A. E. Housman

Nearest Earthly Place to Paradise
The Literary Landscape of Shropshire
   Margaret Wilson and Geoff Taylor

The Temptation and Downfall of the Vicar of Stanton Lacy
   Peter Klien

A Most Rare Vision *Shropshire from the Air* Mark Sisson

Beneath Safer Skies *A Child Evacuee in Shropshire*
   Anthea Toft

It Happened in Shropshire Bob Burrows

Fifty Bales of Hay Roger Evans

A View from the Tractor Roger Evans

A Farmer's Lot Roger Evans

Living off the Land Frances Mountford

My Animals and Other Family Phyllida Barstow

A Job for all Seasons *My Small Country Living*
   Phyllida Barstow

Exraordinary Villages Tony Francis

For more details see: www.merlinunwin.co.uk

Also by Merlin Unwin Books

How the Other Half Lived
A Ludlow's Working Classes 1850-1960
Derek Beattie

Ludlow, Shropshire, is perhaps best known today for its gourmet restaurants, its famous Food Festival and its attractive Georgian and medieval market town centre.

This is a clear-sighted, well presented and fascinating account of the everyday lives of those living on the 'other' side of Ludlow.

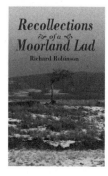

Recollections of a Moorland Lad
Richard Robinson

Withnell Moors in Lancashire appear a lonely wilderness today, to be enjoyed by walkers and wildlife. But only 120 years ago, it was a thriving community and where today piles of moss-covered stones scatter the land, there once stood farms and cottages, green pastures and meadows, all thronging with families who lived, worked and played there.

For more details see: www.merlinunwin.co.uk